IMAGES OF WAR

UNITED STATES ARMY AIRBORNE DIVISIONS 1942-2018

RARE PHOTOGRAPHS FROM WARTIME ARCHIVES

Michael Green

Pen & Sword
MILITARY

First published in Great Britain in 2019 by
PEN & SWORD MILITARY
An imprint of
Pen & Sword Books Ltd
47 Church Street
Barnsley
South Yorkshire
S70 2AS

ISBN 978-1-52673-467-9

Typeset by Concept, Huddersfield, West Yorkshire HD4 5JL.
Printed and bound in China by Printworks Global Ltd.

Pen & Sword Books Limited incorporates the imprints of Atlas, Archaeology, Aviation, Discovery, Family History, Fiction, History, Maritime, Military, Military Classics, Politics, Select, Transport, True Crime, Air World, Frontline Publishing, Leo Cooper, Remember When, Seaforth Publishing, The Praetorian Press, Wharncliffe Local History, Wharncliffe Transport, Wharncliffe True Crime and White Owl.

For a complete list of Pen & Sword titles please contact
PEN & SWORD BOOKS LIMITED
47 Church Street, Barnsley, South Yorkshire S70 2AS, England
E-mail: enquiries@pen-and-sword.co.uk
Website: www.pen-and-sword.co.uk

Contents

Foreword **5**

Acknowledgements **6**

Chapter One
Getting it Together **7**

Chapter Two
Late-War Action **58**

Chapter Three
The Cold War Era **116**

Chapter Four
Post-Cold War **173**

Dedication

The author would like to dedicate this book to the late
Major General William C. Lee,
considered the 'Father of the Airborne'.

Foreword

They were called 'Devils in Baggy Pants', criminals and 'escapees from a lunatic asylum' by their enemies. They brought a new element to warfare: entering battle from the sky by parachute and silent, wooden gliders. They captured the nation's attention with their heroic actions and success over insurmountable odds, at Normandy and at the Battle of the Bulge. Their training was harder and more sadistic than any other unit, they bloused their trousers over their highly-shined jump boots and fought anyone caught doing the same without silver wings on their chest.

These are the airborne soldiers about whom author Michael Green has so deftly written in his latest endeavour for the 'Images of War' series, and this book is an important entry into our historiography of military units, namely airborne divisions. Students of military history have studied the battles and personalities of airborne units either as 'All-Americans' or 'Screaming Eagles'.

United States Army Airborne Divisions is not a book that analyses every intricacy of every battle ever fought by the divisions, although it does cover every major and some minor engagements they fought through current operations. That is not its purpose, which is to provide a road map of the design, composition, changes in capability due to technology, and the partisan and parochial turf battles to develop a Table of Organization and Equipment (TO&E) to man, equip and outfit the division for its intended purpose: to fight and win.

Drawn from interviews and historical army records, the author presents a continual struggle in the early stages of the Second World War to develop highly-specialized units to fill capabilities not found in 'regular' infantry units, compounded with needed replacements and staffing requirements of regular units.

From the Second World War through the Cold War to today's engagements, the author combines compelling text with archival photographs to present to the modern reader an overview of airborne divisions, their history, composition and missions, and looks at how technological advances have changed the structure and missions of the airborne divisions within the US Army.

The words of an old Second World War 'Screaming Eagle' veteran put this book into perspective. He was asked how he could remember so vividly what happened to him in the Second World War. He responded: 'How can I forget?' The latest in the 'Images of War' series pays homage to this old veteran and so many who are no longer with us; we remembered, we didn't forget, and we thank you.

Randy R. Talbot
Command Historian (retired)

Acknowledgements

The historical images in this study come from the National Archives and a number of US Army museum collections. Contemporary pictures came from both various Department of Defense (DOD) image sites and friends.

As with all published works, authors depend on many friends for assistance in reviewing their work and my thanks go to all those involved for their time and patience.

Note to the Reader

Due to space and format restrictions, this work primarily deals with the divisional-level combat activities of the US Army Airborne Divisions in the first two chapters (covering the Second World War) and not combat operations conducted at the regimental or battalion level. The same applies to the Cold War era up through to today, with the emphasis on combat operations and not peace-keeping or humanitarian missions.

Chapter One

Getting it Together

It was the Red Army's groundbreaking work in the mid to late 1930s that articulated both tactics and doctrine for the use of large airborne units (which included parachutists and support military personnel arriving by aircraft) in seizing important objectives behind enemy lines. The German military took notice of the Red Army's work in the field and formed its first airborne division in 1938. In the same period, the US Army paid little serious attention other than experimentally dropping a few men and their weapons by parachute.

The US Army's laissez-faire attitude regarding the opportunities presented by the employment of airborne forces changed in the summer of 1940, with German airborne forces assaulting Belgium and the Netherlands and quickly capturing both a strongly-defended enemy defensive position as well as numerous airfields. They soon established themselves as a fighting elite in the eyes of the world. In response, the US Army formed an airborne platoon (approximately forty men) for field testing.

The Awakening

It was the May 1941 assault by a German airborne division resulting in the capture of the Mediterranean island of Crete that shocked the world. At that time the US Army had only a single airborne battalion in training. Based on its training activities with two airborne battalions in late 1941, the US Army authorized its first airborne parachute infantry regiment (PIR) in March 1942. Referred to as the 'Provisional Parachute Group', it was later relabelled the 'Airborne Command' and in March 1944, reorganized as the 'Airborne Center'.

The Provisional Parachute Group, and later the Airborne Command, were under the command of Colonel William C. Lee. Lee had had a chance before the Second World War to observe a German airborne training exercise. Fascinated, he became a proponent of the US Army forming its airborne forces. His many contributions eventually led to his nickname of the 'Father of the Airborne'.

The US Army's new Airborne Command was tasked to activate, equip and train airborne units for combat. Placed under the direct supervision of Army Ground Forces (AGF), also formed in March 1942, the command reported to Lieutenant General Lesley J. McNair. A three-star general with tremendous influence and support, McNair had mixed feelings about specialized combat types unless he favoured them; i.e. tank destroyers.

Opinions Change

McNair was a firm believer that most specialized combat units were a drain on men and equipment for the US Army. His superior, US Army chief of staff and four-star General George C. Marshall was a strong proponent of such organizations, including the Rangers and Mountain divisions. McNair felt that such units taught only certain skills that he referred to as 'tricks', which in turn led to a decline in their general military proficiency. He felt that a standard infantry division could be reconfigured and provided with necessary training for a specialized task when the need arose.

However, McNair's opinion about airborne divisions began to change. In April 1942, the US Army was already planning the invasion of Western Europe for the spring of 1943. At least one US Army airborne division was envisioned for use in that future operation. Consulting with Airborne Command leadership, McNair became more amenable to the concept of specialized airborne divisions.

Colonel Lee of the Airborne Command visited England the next month to spend time with the British Army 1st Airborne Division, which had been formed in late 1941. So impressed was he that upon his return to the United States, he shared with McNair his enthusiasm for the merits of airborne divisions. The British Army went on to form a second airborne division, the 6th, in 1943.

Airborne Divisions Appear

In June 1942, McNair informed his staff: 'An airborne division should be evolved.' The War Department, the forerunner of the current United States Department of Defense (DOD), approved in late July the formation of two airborne divisions. The new divisions were the 82nd, nicknamed the 'All-Americans' because men from every state were in the ranks, and the 101st 'Screaming Eagles', commemorating Wisconsin regiments during the American Civil War.

Both airborne divisions were created by the conversion of the 82nd Infantry Division. Originally planned as a motorized division, the 82nd Infantry Division reverted to the standard infantry division TO&E during the summer of 1942. It was further split in two, forming the 82nd and 101st Parachute divisions.

McNair had ordered his staff that the forming of airborne divisions should be done 'with a stinginess of overheads and in transportation, which has absolutely no counterpart, thus far in our military establishment'. McNair's preoccupation with austere TO&Es was a hallmark of his time as the head of the AGF and affected both infantry and armoured division TO&Es. In his defence, his major concern was the limited worldwide shipping capacity compared to the shipping requirements of large, equipment-rich specialized divisions.

The Approved Organization

In October 1942 McNair's staff presented a TO&E for the two new airborne divisions, calling for three regiments in each division. Two in each division would be glider infantry regiments (GIRs) of two battalions each, for a total of 1,605 men per regiment. There would also be a single parachute infantry regiment (PIR) composed of three battalions, with a combined total of 1,985 men. Paratroopers were all volunteers, while glider infantrymen were draftees.

Having only two battalions per GIR regiment in the airborne division TO&E was at odds with the rest of the US Army's standard infantry regiments, which had three battalions for an approximate manpower strength of 3,000 per regiment. The major reason for this disparity and in turn the fighting strength of the airborne divisions once on the ground was the limits imposed by the number of aerial assets expected to be available in the future.

Three more US Army airborne divisions eventually formed: the 11th in February 1943, the 17th in April 1943 and the 13th in August 1943. The US Army raised only five US Army airborne divisions compared to the sixty-six infantry divisions fielded during the Second World War, forty-two of which saw action in the ETO and nineteen in the PTO. Sixteen armoured divisions were formed, with none serving in the PTO.

Airborne Division Supporting Elements

To support the three regiments in the October 1942 airborne division TO&E, the two GIRs would each have a battalion of towed 75mm howitzers. The PIR had a single battery of towed 75mm howitzers, air-dropped in pieces and intended to be reassembled on the ground by their crews. These howitzers gave the division hitting power and range for assaults, counter-battery fire and interdicting fire that were simply not possible with man-portable weapons.

The standard US Army infantry division TO&E in 1942 authorized both 105mm and 155mm towed howitzers, but these would have been too large and heavy to be transported by the aerial assets available to the airborne divisions.

The October 1942 TO&E set total airborne divisional manpower at approximately 8,500 men. The regular 1942 infantry division was much larger with an aggregate manpower of approximately 15,000 men. The result was that airborne divisions proved deficient in both administrative and support ranks compared to the standard US Army infantry division, forcing the airborne divisions to rely on their corps-level commands to obtain the support they lacked, which the corps disliked.

Aerial Transport

The glider infantry, unofficially nicknamed the 'Glider Riders', arrived on their objectives in a powerless aircraft designated the CG-4A. Designed by the Weaver Aircraft

Company, the initials of which were 'WACO', these aircraft were sometimes referred to as 'whacko'. The glider's initial test flight took place in May 1942.

The CG-4A's fuselage was constructed of metal tubing and wood, covered by fabric, which was very prone to damage. The wings were all wood, covered by fabric that proved just as flimsy as the fuselage. The CG-4A glider was flown by a two-man crew consisting of pilot and co-pilot, and could carry a maximum of fifteen fully-equipped soldiers.

The construction of the approximately 14,000 units of the CG-4A glider built between late 1942 and 1945 was besieged by production delays and serious quality control issues. This could be attributed to the fact that the manufacturing contracts for the glider went to sixteen firms inexperienced in the construction of aircraft.

Of those CG-4A gliders that came off the factory floor, about 6,000 reached the European Theatre of Operations (ETO), 2,000 went to the Mediterranean Theatre of Operations and 500 to the Pacific Theatre of Operations (PTO).

As they arrived overseas unassembled in crates, the CG-4A gliders had to be reassembled, often by low-skilled personnel, which left a large number of them unusable. Many of those shipped to North Africa in early 1943 were found to have their wooden components warped due to the heat in that part of the world.

When assigned to transport a single 75mm towed artillery piece or a single 0.25-ton 4 × 4 truck (Jeep), the passenger count of the CG-4A glider was greatly reduced. Two additional wartime glider designs were eventually put into production, but arrived overseas too late to see use in combat.

The CG-4A glider was towed to its objectives by the twin-engine 'C-47 Skytrain', a militarized version of the pre-war commercial DC-3 passenger plane, which could carry up to eighteen fully-equipped paratroopers. Employed late in the Second World War to supplement the C-47 was the larger twin-engine 'C-46 Commando', also a modified pre-war commercial passenger plane design. It could carry as many as forty fully-equipped paratroopers.

All the aircraft and gliders, as well as their flight crews, belonged to the Troop Carrier Command (TCC) formed in June 1942. It, in turn, was responsible to the US Army Air Forces (USAAF) established in June 1941 and not the AGF under McNair's command. Below the level of the Troop Carrier Command were Troop Carrier Groups, subdivided into Troop Carrier Wings and then into squadrons.

Into Combat

Not everybody in the Airborne Command concurred with the October 1942 TO&E. Once overseas the airborne division's organization began to change unofficially; this was due to factors outside of their control. The initial example of this occurred before Operation HUSKY, the Allied military invasion of Sicily in July 1943.

The 82nd Airborne was assigned to the US Army portion of Operation HUSKY. Due to a shortage of functional CG-4A gliders, the division had two reinforced PIRs and a single GIR, the opposite of the authorized October 1942 airborne division TO&E.

Before the 9 July 1943 nighttime parachute drop by 226 aircraft of the 52nd Troop Carrier Wing, the leading element of Operation HUSKY, the then Colonel James M. Gavin prepared a written message handed to his men before climbing onto their transport planes. An extract reads: 'The term "American parachutist" has become synonymous with courage of the highest order. Let us carry the fight to the enemy and make the American parachutist feared and respected through all his ranks. Attack violently. Destroy him wherever found.'

The 82nd's introduction to combat during Operation HUSKY was not the success hoped for by the US Army. Plans had called for a single reinforced PIR of the division to drop onto Sicily the night before the main amphibious assault began. Its objective was the high ground 5 miles inland from the US Army's invasion beachhead at the Sicilian Gulf of Gela. Once in position, it was expected to disrupt anticipated German and Italian counter-attacks on the landing beaches to be assaulted the next morning by three US Army infantry divisions.

Not Going to Plan

A combination of factors led to the actual nighttime airdrop of one of the two PIRs of the 82nd Airborne Division over Sicily turning into a major fiasco. The 52nd Troop Carrier Wing pilots assigned were ill-trained. Flying over a large body of water (the Mediterranean) to reach the island of Sicily was something they had never done and for which they weren't prepared. It required navigation skill and equipment not present at the time. The weather also proved much worse than anticipated and soon broke up the tight-knit aerial formations that had taken off from airfields in North Africa.

The widely-dispersed and bewildered pilots, trying to find Sicily in the darkness, were forced to depend on dead reckoning or in some cases just pure luck to locate the island. Once over the island, they had to peer through smoke from the pre-invasion naval bombardments and avoid enemy anti-aircraft fire at the same time. The result of all their confusion was that the 82nd's single reinforced PIR landed almost everywhere but where intended. Out of the 3,405 men of the 82nd Division's reinforced PIR dropped over Sicily on the night of 9 July, only 425 landed on their assigned objective. Some found themselves over 65 miles away from the drop point. Colonel Gavin, nicknamed 'Jumping Jim', landed 25 miles away from the objective and walked back to take command of his men that had landed on the objective.

In late July 1943, two-star Major General Matthew Ridgway, commander of the 82nd Airborne Division, stated that the operation 'demonstrated beyond any doubt that the Air Force … cannot at present put parachute units, even as large as a battalion, within effective attack distance of a chosen drop zone at night'.

Friendly Fire Takes its Toll

Adding to the 82nd's misfortunes during Operation HUSKY was another calamity, which occurred on the night of 11 July. To reinforce the original PIR on the ground for the night of 9 July, the second PIR of the division came in for support. Unfortunately, the flight path of these reinforcements took them directly over the US Navy invasion fleet off Gela and the US Army units already ashore, which had already been subjected to a series of deadly aerial attacks by both the German and Italian Air Forces before their arrival on the scene.

When the scared young sailors and US Army anti-aircraft gunners heard the 140 C-47s of the 52nd Troop Carrier Wing approaching their positions, they assumed that it was another enemy attack and opened fire. In their panic, they shot down twenty-three C-47s and seriously damaged thirty-seven others. Some 81 paratroopers were killed, with 132 wounded and another 16 missing. Among the troop carrier wing personnel, 7 aircrew members were killed, with another 30 wounded and 53 missing.

One airborne officer would later write:

It was a most uncomfortable feeling knowing that our own troops were throwing everything they had at us. Planes dropped out of formation and crashed into the sea. Others, like clumsy whales, wheeled and attempted to get beyond the flak which rose in fountains of fire, lighting the stricken faces of men as they stared through the windows.

In some cases, those C-47s that went into the water near the US Navy invasion fleet or crash-landed on Sicily remained under fire before it painfully dawned on those doing the firing that they were shooting at fellow Americans. One pilot in serious jest would state that 'Evidently the safest place for us tonight while over Sicily would have been over enemy territory.'

A landing by the single GIR of the 82nd in Sicily planned for the following night was quickly cancelled due to what had happened to the 2nd PIR, as well as the poor results of a British Army glider operation conducted over Sicily on the night of 11 July. Of the 144 British Army gliders that took part, ninety crashed into the sea, thirty-two along the Sicilian coast, and only twelve reached their assigned landing zone. The GIR of the 82nd eventually reached Sicily by sea and not by glider delivery.

Ridgway had rightly feared that flying at night over the US Navy invasion fleet off Sicily was a disaster waiting to happen. As such, he had confronted his army and navy superiors about the danger of such an arrangement. He, in turn, had been repeatedly reassured that it would not be a problem. A major investigation was quickly ordered to uncover what had gone wrong on the night of 11 July. In the end, no blame was assigned to anybody and the entire unfortunate incident was to go down as a painful lesson learned.

Follow-On Activities

Following the conclusion of Operation HUSKY, there were plans to employ the 82nd in some additional operations. The most ambitious of these called for the division to seize an airfield near the Italian capital of Rome from which they could secure the city. It, like so many other plans for the division, would quickly fall by the wayside as Lieutenant General Mark Clark, commander of the Fifth Army, decided not to deploy the division in the initial invasion of Italy, Operation AVALANCHE, which began on 9 September 1943 at Salerno.

Clark would change his mind about the need for the 82nd as strong German counter-attacks threatened his beachhead positions on 13 September. In response, two of the division's PIRs were successfully air-dropped into the existing Salerno beachhead as reinforcements that same evening. The drop of the third PIR of the division, hurriedly assigned an objective behind German lines, failed miserably, with some of its paratroopers deposited approximately 40 miles from their intended drop zone.

The Reckoning

On a larger scale, the mixed success of the US Army airborne operations during Operation HUSKY and the early stages of Operation AVALANCHE caused many to doubt their future viability. Dwight D. Eisenhower, who would go on to become Supreme Allied Commander Allied Expeditionary Force in January 1944, would express his doubt about the future of airborne divisions in a letter to General George C. Marshall, Chief of Staff of the US Army, on 23 September 1943. An extract from that letter reads: 'I do not believe in the airborne division. I believe that airborne troops should be reorganized in self-contained units … all about the size of a regimental combat team.'

Based on the poor results of the airborne portion of Operation HUSKY, McNair's early doubts about the requirement for airborne divisions resurfaced. In an extract from a memo, McNair stated: 'I was prepared to recommend to the War Department that airborne divisions be abandoned in our scheme of organization and that airborne effort be restricted to parachute units of battalion size or smaller.'

In the aftermath of Operations HUSKY and AVALANCHE, two formal investigations were convened by the US Army to determine if the concept of airborne divisions had any future. One was headed by Brigadier General Albert Pierson, assistant divisional commander of the newly-formed 11th Airborne Division, the other by Major General Joseph M. Swing, the senior airborne advisor to those who planned Operation HUSKY and appointed as the commander of the 11th.

One Last Chance

Before the airborne division investigations ended, McNair held a large-scale training exercise in the United States by the 11th, as it had not yet gone overseas. The training exercise was referred to as the 'Knollwood Manoeuvres', and it took place between 5 and 12 December 1943 with many senior officers present. Marshall believed in the value of airborne divisions but felt that everybody needed more training time.

Approximately 10,000 US Army personnel took part in the Knollwood Manoeuvres, with 4,679 paratroopers delivered by approximately 200 C-47s during a nighttime air-drop and another 1,869 by a fleet of 234 CG-4A gliders on 7 December. Also another 3,774 men were transported by aircraft to a so-called captured airport as reinforcements for those who had already arrived by parachute or gliders.

Upon the conclusion of the manoeuvres, Major General Swing prepared a report on the results which he submitted to McNair. To everybody's surprise, McNair wrote back to Swing on 16 December 1943, stating that '[t]he successful performance of your division has convinced me that we were wrong, and I shall now recommend that we continue our present schedule of activating, training, and committing airborne divisions.' McNair's endorsement of the airborne division to the War Department secured its role as a continuing part of the US Army.

Unofficial Changes to the TO&E

Elements of the 101st began arriving in Great Britain in October 1943 and elements of the 82nd in November 1943. Upon arrival, they both began preparing themselves for their part in what became known as Operation NEPTUNE, the first phase of Operation OVERLORD, launched on 6 June 1944. The latter was the overall name assigned to the establishment of a large-scale presence by the Western Allies on the continent of Europe.

In November 1943, Ridgway, still commander of the 82nd, was extremely concerned about the airborne divisions' austere October 1942 TO&E that had been imposed by McNair. He believed that this left them at a serious disadvantage when committed to combat in France, so sought a dramatic increase in their man-power and equipment levels. His thoughts were echoed by those at the most senior level of the ETO. However, McNair objected and the proposed changes were not approved.

In February 1944, McNair allowed some minor tweaking of the original October 1942 airborne division TO&E. However, at this point, it still called for an airborne division to have two GIRs and a single PIR, which was not the reality then in place.

Changes in Organizations and Personnel

With Eisenhower's unofficial approval, the increase in manpower and equipment for the 82nd and 101st went ahead anyway. Instead of having two GIRs and a single PIR, both divisions would go into combat with a much more robust arrangement.

By the time of Operation NEPTUNE, the 82nd had a four-regiment arrangement, with three PIRs and a single GIR. The 101st had a five-regiment arrangement, with three PIRs and two GIRs. Also both divisions' GIRs were increased from the authorized two-battalion structure to three battalions, bringing their manpower strength up to the same approximate levels as the PIRs.

In March 1944, Major General Maxwell D. Taylor replaced Major General Lee as commander of the 101st. Lee, having suffered a heart attack, was evacuated to the United States and eventually medically retired from the US Army. Lee died in 1948 at the age of 53.

Preparing for the Invasion

To transport the 82nd and 101st to France for Operation NEPTUNE, the USAAF formed the IX Troop Carrier Command in October 1943. It had more than 900 aircraft and approximately 500 gliders. Due to a continuing shortage of CG-4A gliders, more than 300 British-designed and built gliders named the 'Horsa' entered into the IX Troop Carrier Command's inventory before Operation NEPTUNE. Larger than their American counterparts, the Horsas could carry more passengers and equipment.

To avoid a repeat of the friendly-fire incident that had occurred over Sicily during Operation HUSKY, the aircraft of IX Troop Carrier Command flew around the Allied invasion fleet heading towards the French coast in the early-morning darkness of 6 June. In addition, all aircraft and gliders received three whitewashed stripes on their wings to denote them as friendly. Unfortunately, the convoluted flight path caused navigational problems for some of the pilots, which were compounded by other factors when they reached the French coast.

The final role assigned to the approximately 13,000 men of the 82nd and 101st was to secure objectives inland the night before the approximately 14,000 men of the US Army 4th Infantry Division began landing on Utah Beach. The reason for a night-time airborne operation had to do with the US Army's continued belief that a certain degree of darkness (during moonlit nights) provided a level of concealment from both enemy aerial and ground forces during the very vulnerable landing phase of the airborne operation.

To aid the pilots of IX Troop Carrier Command in finding their nighttime objectives, the US Army airborne divisions employed small groups of parachutists referred to as 'pathfinders'. They would arrive just before the main air-drops to deploy a variety of electronic and visual devices to guide the pilots to the correct drop zones.

The concept of pathfinders was conceived and put into practice by the 82nd following Operation HUSKY.

Glider Operations

Glider landings involving both airborne divisions were to take place in the early-morning darkness of 6 June and at dusk the same day. They brought with them 4 × 4 0.25-ton trucks (Jeeps), the divisions' artillery and anti-tank guns, as well as long-range communication gear. It was assumed that the PIRs would have secured the gliders' landing zones.

As there was a shortage of glider pilots and towing aircraft, some of the GIR elements would arrive by sea. There were also two additional glider landings planned for 7 June. In total, approximately 4,000 men were to be brought in by gliders between 6 and 7 June.

Richard H. Denison, a C-47 pilot of the IX Troop Carrier Command, describes his impression of the glider pilots:

> [They] were an unusual breed of men. Every time you made a glider landing, it was a controlled crash, and you were committed; there was no return ... Upon talking with these people, later on, I found them bitter, difficult to manage and simply no compunction about telling the commander or any officer to go to hell. They would say, 'Okay court-martial us, and you may save our lives.'

The Best-Laid Plans of Mice and Men

In spite of the extensive preparations and training conducted before Operation NEPTUNE, the divisional-sized airborne activities that were such a key part of the invasion force failed to live up to their expectations. The reasons were the same as had befallen the 82nd during Operation HUSKY. These included the fact that the troop carrier pilots remained poorly-trained for the difficult tasks they were assigned, the immaturity of the existing night navigation technology and unexpected weather conditions.

The most important goal of the troop carrier pilots in the darkness during the very early hours of 6 June was to maintain their tight-knit tactical formations, referred to as 'serials'. Only by remaining in tight serials over the 'drop zone' in the case of para-troopers or the 'landing zone' for gliders could there be any hope of the troops landing en masse on their chosen objectives. For the small number of pathfinders being sent into France first, the troop carrier pilots flew in serials of no more than three aircraft. For the PIRs and those that followed, a serial could include up to fifty aircraft.

When the first serials (carrying the pathfinders) began taking off from England shortly before midnight on 5/6 June, they had optimum weather conditions.

Unfortunately, as they neared the French coast, they and all the following serials encountered the same dense cloud bank, high winds and enemy anti-aircraft fire. This unnerved many of the pilots who, fearing mid-air collisions, quickly took violent evasive actions, resulting in many of the serials breaking up and leaving individual pilots to find their objectives on their own.

Those pathfinders that did land on their assigned drop zones had been unable to deploy their navigational aids, in most cases due to the presence of nearby enemy troop formations. What they failed to do with the initial paratrooper drops, they made up for by marking the later glider landing zones.

The Results

Of the two airborne divisions, the paratroopers of the 82nd found themselves more widely scattered over the French countryside than those of the 101st, allowing the latter to complete some of its assigned missions on 6 June. Despite being able to assemble only 2,500 of the 6,600 men it committed to battle, the 82nd was able to secure only one of its first-day objectives, having been able to marshal only 40 per cent of its manpower and 10 per cent of its artillery.

Lee Griffing, a paratrooper of the 101st, remembers a German anti-aircraft vehicle trying to shoot him out of the sky as he floated down to the French countryside:

> I was coming down on a flak wagon [anti-aircraft vehicle], and I was the only thing they had to shoot at. Tracers went under me, and I pulled my legs up. Then they went over me. As the ground came up, I had to make a decision about what kind of landing to make – a ground landing, a tree landing, or a water landing. If you make the right decision, you walk away. If you make the wrong one, you break a leg, or you drown. What I saw below me was so uniform that it just had to be grass or low scrubs. The flak wagon was slightly behind me. So, I pulled on my front risers and slipped the chute forward to get as far away as I could from the flak wagon, and landed maybe a hundred feet from it … The flak wagon gave up shooting at me [on the ground] to shoot at the [incoming] planes.

Only 10 per cent of the paratroopers from the two airborne divisions landed on their assigned drop zones, with up to 30 per cent landing within a radius of a mile and another 20 per cent between 1 and 2 miles of the drop zone.

However, the wide dispersal of the US Army paratroopers on 6 June may have proved somewhat fortuitous, as the Germans inflicted heavy casualties on the airborne battalions that had landed en masse on their assigned objectives. Overall losses among the paratroopers on 6 June was over 50 per cent, which was thankfully below the 70 per cent loss rate predicted by a senior British officer.

The glider landings for both airborne divisions on 6 June were also as scattered as those of the paratroopers, with heavy losses in equipment but thankfully less so in personnel. Leonard Lebenson, a glider infantryman of the 82nd, remembers the experience of landing in France:

> Then we suddenly knew we were flying on our own. In other words, we weren't being towed any more; we had been cut loose. That is a very unusual feeling, flying through the air without a motor. It's noiseless. All you hear is the rushing sound of the air, but other than that it's very quiet … Then there was a sudden up movement on the aircraft – like a little elevator uplift; you could feel it pancaking. Then we hit something, and then again … We hit a tree, bounced off a shed, and landed against another tree. Pieces of the gliders were strewn over a relatively small field. But the fourteen men climbed out of the wreckage. Only one guy was hurt. Hurray! We're in France!

The Ending

Accepted US Army airborne division doctrine of that time called for relatively quick withdrawal once ground troops reached the positions the division had seized in battle. This did not occur due to a shortage of infantry divisions, a problem that would bedevil the US Army throughout the fighting in the ETO. Instead, the 82nd and 101st remained on the front lines until July 1944.

The 82nd was relieved on 8 July 1944 and the 101st on 10 July 1944. At that point, the divisions returned to England for rest and refitting so they could prepare for their next airborne operation. It was during this time that the 82nd, but not the 101st, reverted back to a three-regimental structure.

New Command Structures

The 82nd and 101st were transferred to the command of the First Allied Airborne Army (FAAA), formed on 16 July 1944, but not officially labelled until 16 August 1944. Command of the FAAA went to Lieutenant General Lewis H. Brereton, formerly in charge of the Ninth US Air Force. Second-in-command of the FAAA went to a British officer.

Besides the airborne divisions, the FAAA took charge of the Troop Carrier Command in the ETO, which had previously been under the command of the USAAF. The FAAA was not a combat command; rather it was a headquarters unit that oversaw planning for future airborne operations and training of the airborne divisions in the ETO.

On 25 August 1944, the 82nd and 101st were brought together under the command of the newly-established 'XVIII Airborne Corps', which was a headquarters unit subordinate to the FAAA. Appointed commander of the new airborne corps was Ridgway, the former divisional commander of the 82nd.

The US Army formed a total of twenty-four corps during the Second World War, which typically consisted of two infantry divisions and a single armoured division, but in theory could command any mixture of divisions from two to five. Armies commanded two or more corps.

A classic image of early-war German paratroopers going into action. Visible are their trademark brimless helmets and one-piece jump smocks. The latter were designed to prevent any part of their clothing or equipment being caught on the aircraft's fuselage as they exited. It also prevented their uniforms from becoming entangled in the parachute shroud lines when they deployed. (*National Archives*)

(**Above**) The original uniform for the US Army's paratroopers consisted of a one-piece herringbone twill mechanic's coverall as seen on the paratroopers pictured here. The majority of parachutists pictured are wearing only their larger main parachutes and harness and not the smaller reserve chute that fitted to the front of their harness. Neither British nor German paratroopers had reserve chutes. (*National Archives*)

(**Opposite, above left**) An experimental uniform item designed for US Army paratroopers as seen here was a one-piece overall made of satin that had zippered pockets accessible by the paratroopers while wearing their parachutes and harnesses. As it was shown to retain a great deal of body heat, it quickly disappeared from service. The parachute visible is the T-4, identified by the vertical orientation of the front reserve chute. (*National Archives*)

(**Opposite, above right**) For an added degree of protection upon landing, early US Army paratroopers wore a modified plastic football helmet as pictured. The modifications included a leather one-piece, moulded cup-style chin-strap to prevent on-rushing air pulling the helmet off when the paratrooper was descending. The second modification pictured was a leather covering over the parachutist's throat to protect him when landing in trees or thick shrubbery. (*National Archives*)

(**Opposite, below**) In this image we see a US Army paratrooper exiting a US Army Air Force (USAAF) C-38 twin-engine transport plane. The army acquired thirty-five units of the aircraft between 1938 and 1939. The paratrooper in the picture is shown clutching his manually-operated front reserve chute as the static line (attached to the plane) is almost completely run out and will automatically pull out his main chute canopy worn on his back. (*National Archives*)

(**Opposite, above**) Pictured in the peaked cap talking to an umpire during a war game held in the United States in 1942 is Lieutenant General Lesley J. McNair, the head of the US Army Ground Forces (AGF). He was tasked with the organization and training of all the different types of divisions deployed overseas, including the airborne divisions. The senior leadership of the airborne divisions seldom agreed with the TO&Es imposed by McNair. (*National Archives*)

(**Above**) Reflecting the difficult roles assigned to US Army paratroopers, only the fittest were chosen, with constant physical conditioning being a normal routine when not in combat. Nobody found themselves drafted into the airborne during the Second World War. You were either recruited or transferred in from another type of unit. As the airborne was seen by many as the elite of the army, it never lacked volunteers. (*National Archives*)

(**Opposite, below**) When those aspiring to be paratroopers completed basic training, they would go on to 'Jump School'. It was here that they learned all the specialized skills needed to perform the role. This included learning how to pack their main and reserve parachutes as well as control them once they landed. To provide a degree of realism when learning the latter skill, Hollywood wind machines, seen here, were used. (*National Archives*)

To prepare trainees for the physical sensation of hurling themselves out of a plane in freefall and the shock from their main parachutes being automatically deployed by a static line, the US Army purchased a number of large 'jump towers', originally designed and built as amusement rides for the 1939 World's Fair in New York City. They were disassembled, shipped and rebuilt at Fort Bragg, North Carolina, the long-time home of the US Army's airborne divisions. (*National Archives*)

(**Above, left**) As the paratrooper's original modified plastic football helmet lacked any ballistic protection, the US Army approved production of the replacement M1 steel helmet in 1941, seen in this image. The helmet itself consisted of a 3mm steel outer shell and an inner plastic liner, which contained an adjustable suspension system. Both the helmet and liner were kept on a soldier's head by two-piece canvas chin-straps. (*National Archives*)

(**Above, right**) To provide a sturdier helmet arrangement for paratroopers that would not come off when leaving an aircraft or during descent, there appeared two modified versions of the M1 helmet: the M2 seen here and the almost identical M1C in December 1944. Both retained the two-piece, canvas chin-strap for the helmet but also added a one-piece leather cup-style, moulded chin-strap, attached to the plastic liner with a more elaborate adjustable suspension strapping system. (*National Archives*)

(**Left**) In this steely-eyed artist's portrayal of a paratrooper wearing the M2 helmet also referred to as the 'D-Bale', we see a bit more of the A-frame strapping arrangement aimed at keeping the plastic liner and helmet on his head. The artist painted the subject armed with the .30 Calibre Carbine M1A1, fitted with a folding stock designed specifically for paratroopers. (*National Archives*)

Become a Paratrooper

(**Right**) The re-enactor pictured here has two identifying uniform features common to US Army paratroopers in the ETO until the latter part of 1944. Number one is the dark brown leather laced 10in jump boots, also known as 'paratrooper boots'. The second is the M1942 lightweight tan-coloured, two-piece 'jump suit' consisting of blouse and trousers. The trousers had large cargo pockets, which the standard-issue infantrymen's trousers did not have. (*Ian Wilcox*)

(**Opposite, above**) Armed with an M1903A4 Sniper Rifle is a re-enactor wearing the M1942 paratrooper tan jump suit. It was made from a cotton twill material that was both windproof and waterproof. The trousers' upper thigh inseams came with cloth leg tapes to allow the paratroopers to tie down the items stored in his trouser cargo pockets. The trench knife attached to his ankle is historically accurate. (*Ian Wilcox*)

(**Opposite, below left**) Unlike the standard infantryman's 1941 Parsons field jacket that had only two exterior cuff pockets, the M1942 paratrooper jump suit had two exterior slanted cargo breast pockets and two exterior thigh cargo pockets, as seen with this re-enactor. As the light shade of the 1942 jump suit was considered unsuitable for the ETO, some paratroopers sprayed on alternating shades of dark paint to better disguise themselves prior to Operation NEPTUNE, as has this re-enactor. (*Ian Wilcox*)

(**Opposite, below right**) A US Army paratrooper is shown performing a last-minute inspection of a fellow parachutist's T-5 main chute and attached harness. British Army parachutes and harnesses of the Second World War came with a quick-release mechanism. The US Army feared that its paratroopers might accidentally open their main chutes when descending and fall out of their harnesses to their death, and therefore the T-5 lacked such a release. (*National Archives*)

(**Above**) Laid out for inspection are some of the many items of kit that individual paratroopers carried into combat. Notice the bipod just below the two parachutes; that identifies the paratrooper as being part of a six-man 60mm mortar team. The bipod lies on its canvas carrying-case. As this kit belongs to a paratrooper serving in the Pacific Theatre of Operation (PTO) he has a machete, not seen in the ETO. (*National Archives*)

(**Opposite, above left**) The paratroopers pictured here are wearing the 1942 jumpsuit as is evident by the tan colour of their uniforms and the thigh cargo pockets with tie-down straps. Underneath their parachutes and harnesses can be seen the yellow Type-B4 inflatable lifejackets that had to be worn if they were to transit over water. Note also the T-shaped handle of their M1910 entrenching tool. (*National Archives*)

(**Opposite, above right**) The paratrooper in this photograph is shown with the single-piece, 54in-long M1A1 Rocket-Launcher, commonly referred to by its unofficial nickname of the 'Bazooka'. Visible on this paratrooper's front waist is the M1936 Musette field bag. On the paratrooper's thigh, the dark-coloured bag is a black rubberized canvas carrying-case for the M5 Gas Mask. (*National Archives*)

(**Opposite, below**) In this image we see a paratrooper crouching with his submachine gun prepared to deal with an imaginary enemy. During training, white T-5 main chutes were employed as seen in this photograph. During combat jumps, a dark-coloured camouflaged pattern T-5 main parachute was employed. Originally made of silk, by late 1943 they were constructed of nylon. The reserve chutes were always white. (*National Archives*)

they've got the GUTS

GIVE 'EM MORE FIREPOWER

(**Above**) In this dramatically-composed wartime poster aimed at encouraging increased production by civilian war workers, we see two paratroopers having just landed. The submachine gun is the M1928A1 Thompson, commonly referred to by its unofficial nickname of the 'Tommy Gun'. Unfortunately, the artist painted that figure with a rifle cartridge belt. Note that the gas mask container seems a bit oversized. (*National Archives*)

(**Opposite, above**) The transportation workhorse of the United Army Air Forces (USAAF) in the Second World War was the C-47 Skytrain pictured here. Commonly referred to by its unofficial nickname of the 'Gooney Bird', it was adapted from the DC-3 commercial airliner that had first appeared in service in 1936. C-47s flew paratroopers to their objectives and towed the gliders to their landing zones, with approximately 10,000 built during the war years. (*Department of Defense*, hereafter *DOD*)

(**Opposite, below**) With a crew of four, the C-47 Skytrain was capable of carrying up to eighteen combat-equipped paratroopers or approximately 8,000lb of cargo. It had a maximum speed of 232mph, with a typical cruising speed of 175mph. When tasked with dropping paratroopers it could lower its speed to about 110mph. There was a two-piece fuselage door on the left-hand side of the aircraft. (*National Archives*)

(**Above**) The cockpit of a C-47 Skytrain. The crew of four in theory consisted of a pilot, co-pilot, navigator and radio operator. Aircraft range was about 1,500 miles with a service ceiling of approximately 24,000ft. Paratroopers were typically dropped at under 1,000ft. Those C-47s and aircrew assigned to carrying paratroopers and towing gliders belonged to the Troop Carrier Command (TCC) which was formed in June 1942. (*USAF Museum*)

(**Opposite, above**) The paratroopers in this C-47 Skytrain are wearing a slightly modified version of the army's new universal two-piece 1943 standard field uniform, which consisted of a hip-length jacket, patterned on the paratroopers' 1942 two-piece jump suit, and new over-trousers. Both were made from a dark green smooth sateen cotton cloth. As of late 1944, it had completely replaced the 1942 two-piece tan jump suit. (*National Archives*)

(**Opposite, below**) Beginning in 1942, the United Army Air Forces (USAAF) took into service the C-46 Commando pictured here. Like the C-47 Skytrain, it was based on a commercial passenger plane design. The Troop Carrier Command (TCC) in the ETO would not employ the Commando for transporting paratroopers until early 1945. As it was larger and more powerful, it could carry more paratroopers or cargo than the Skytrain. (*USAF Museum*)

(**Opposite, above**) Approximately 3,000 units of the C-46 Commando were built during the Second World War. The fuselage was large enough to transport a 0.25-ton truck as seen in this museum diorama. The version employed by the TCC in early 1945 was designated the C-46D and was specially modified with two single-piece doors on either side of the fuselage, optimized for paratroopers. (*USAF Museum*)

(**Above**) The cockpit of a C-46 Commando. The aircraft lacked the self-sealing fuel tanks that had been retro-fitted to the C-47 Skytrain fleet of the TCC in the ETO by early 1945. When flying low and slow when tasked as a paratrooper transport aircraft in early 1945, it proved easy prey for German anti-aircraft gunners. It was subsequently banned from future airborne operations for that reason. (*USAF Museum*)

(**Opposite, below**) An important part of every US Army airborne division during the Second World War was its glider infantry regiment (GIR). The men that served in these regiments were transported to their objectives by the CG-4A glider seen here, which could carry up to fifteen fully-equipped soldiers. Weighing about 7,500lb, the maximum towing speed of the CG-4A proved to be 120mph. (*USAF Museum*)

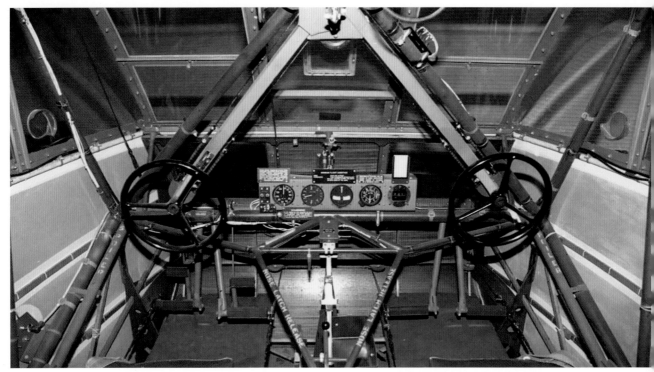

The cockpit of a CG-4A glider. Unlike the powered USAAF aircraft flown by commissioned officers, gliders were typically flown by non-commissioned officers (NCOs) of the USAAF who, upon completing glider training, were labelled 'flight officers'. Some glider pilots were those who had failed conventional pilot training for powered aircraft. (*USAF Museum*)

Gliders, like the CG-4A pictured here, were released from their tow-planes at varying altitudes down to 400ft. It was originally envisioned that the CG-4A glider could be reusable. However, in practice this proved unworkable as most were so badly damaged during landing that they were not worth saving. In such cases they were typically stripped of anything useful and burned in situ. (*USAF Museum*)

Due to the size and weight restrictions of the C-47 Skytrain, the bulk of the airborne division's heavier equipment went by CG-4A gliders, including the 4 × 4 0.25-ton truck (Jeep) seen here. Unlike the paratroopers, the glider infantrymen had no specialized uniform items. They wore the standard infantryman's uniform and ankle boots, with canvas leggings, as seen on the soldier in the foreground. (*National Archives*)

(**Opposite, above**) In this picture we see a size comparison between a C-47 Skytrain and a CG-4A glider. In training exercises, it was proved that a single Skytrain could tow two gliders at the same time, with the gliders having different lengths of tow ropes. However, this was considered too dangerous to be employed at night, so it was not tested in combat by the US Army until early 1945. (*USAF Museum*)

(**Above**) The heaviest authorized artillery piece for the US Army airborne divisions was the 75mm M1A1 Pack Howitzer. An example is seen here, having just fired a blank round for the movie camera visible on the far right of the photograph. The 1,269lb howitzer had a maximum firing range of approximately 10,000 yards. There were thirty-six in the TO&E of the 1942 airborne division. (*National Archives*)

(**Opposite, below**) The 75mm M1A1 Pack Howitzers of the airborne divisions could be transported to their objectives by two different methods. The first approach was by CG-4A glider as seen here, with its crew sitting on removable wooden benches on either side of the fuselage. The alternative was by disassembling the weapon into nine separate pieces that could be air-dropped from a C-47 Skytrain and then reassembled by its crew at the drop zone. (*National Archives*)

Each 1942 TO&E Parachute Infantry Regiment (PIR) called for 132 units of the M1917A4 air-cooled .30 calibre machine gun as pictured in this training exercise photograph. They were divided between the PIR's three infantry battalions, which had 495 men each. The .30 calibre machine gun was operated by a crew of three: gunner, assistant gunner and ammo bearer. *(National Archives)*

Each of the two GIRs in the planned 1942 airborne division's regimental TO&E was authorized eight of the water-cooled .30 calibre machine gun M1917A1 pictured here. It was classified as a heavy machine gun. The word 'heavy' was a relative term. It was labelled a heavy machine gun only because it was less mobile than the M1917A4 air-cooled .30 calibre version. *(National Archives)*

Airborne divisions in their 1942 TO&E had a total of 109 air-cooled M2-HB .50 calibre machine guns authorized. The division artillery had the bulk of them with fifty-six units, with thirty-six belonging to the single anti-aircraft battalion that divided them among three batteries. The remaining seventeen were divided among other elements of the division. The 1944 airborne division TO&E authorized a total of 165 air-cooled M2-HB .50 calibre machine guns. *(National Archives)*

When the airborne division TO&E of 1942 was formalized, it authorized forty-four units of the 37mm light anti-tank gun M3A1 pictured here. The division artillery had four, each of the two GIRs had eight and the division's misnamed anti-aircraft battalion had twenty-four. Unlike the 75mm M1A1 Pack Howitzers which could be broken down into pieces for parachute delivery, the 37mm light anti-tank gun M3A1 had to be glider-delivered. *(Pierre-Olivier Buan)*

(**Above**) Combat experience gained by the US Army in early 1943 showed that the 37mm light anti-tank gun M3A1 was obsolete. This led the airborne divisions to replace them with the British Army Ordnance Quick-Firing 6-Pounder (57mm) anti-tank gun as seen here, beginning in early 1944. The version adopted by the airborne divisions was mounted on a narrower and lighter carriage designated the Mk III, designed specifically for glider use by British industry. (*Ian Wilcox*)

(**Opposite**) What is interesting in this picture of a British Army 6-Pounder (57mm) anti-tank gun being loaded in a US Army CG-4A glider are the skids seen under the raised cockpit nose and fuselage. These allowed the glider to skid across hard ground. Conversely, they could dig into soft ground and bring the glider to an abrupt halt, causing internal cargo to break its hold-downs and crush the glider's occupants. (*National Archives*)

(**Right**) In March 1945, a small number of the brand-new M18 57mm Recoilless Rifles arrived in the ETO, with the airborne divisions having priority to acquire them. In anticipation of their use by the airborne divisions, specialized air-droppable containers were developed for the weapon and its associated tripod and ammunition. As seen in this post-war image, the recoilless rifle could also be fired from the shoulder. (*National Archives*)

(**Above**) Supplementing the M18 57mm Recoilless Rifles in the service of the airborne divisions in the ETO in early 1945 was a small number of M20 75mm Recoilless Rifles. Due to the weapon's size and weight it could only be fired from a ground tripod, as seen here. As with the M18 57mm Recoilless Rifle, the M20 fired both a high-explosive (HE) round as well as a high-explosive anti-tank (HEAT) round. (*National Archives*)

(**Opposite, above**) The airborne division TO&E of October 1942 called for 233 units of the two-wheel hand cart designated the M3A4. In addition, there were authorized twenty units of the almost identical two-wheel hand cart M6A1, which was intended to carry the 81mm mortar or as an ammunition cart for other weapons. The type of hand cart being moved by the paratrooper pictured here is unknown. (*National Archives*)

(**Opposite, below**) To minimize the number of vehicles that had to be transported by the CG-4A gliders of the airborne divisions and still provide the divisions' personnel with some degree of mobility once on the ground, each division was authorized 205 motor scooters in the October 1942 TO&E. A restored example is seen here, with an attached two-wheel handcart. Despite being authorized in 1942, the motor scooters were not available until 1944. (*USAF Museum*)

(**Opposite, above**) If the C-47 Skytrain could be considered the aerial workhorse of the US Army during the Second World War, then its ground counterpart was the 6 × 6 2.5-ton Cargo Truck Standard pictured here, commonly referred to by its unofficial nickname of the 'Deuce and a Half'. The October 1942 airborne division TO&E called for eighty-five of them. They were not air-transportable. To increase the trucks' carrying capacity the division was authorized a total of 100 1-ton two-wheel towed trailers. (*Pierre-Olivier Buan*)

(**Opposite, below**) The engineer battalion of the 1942 airborne division TO&E called for four glider-transportable crawler tractors. The type employed is seen here and was designated the CA-1 Airborne Tractor/Bulldozer. It was powered by a four-cylinder gasoline engine, and besides the hydraulically-operated bulldozer blade, was equipped with a winch at the rear of the vehicle, which does not appear on the example shown here. (*USAF Museum*)

(**Above**) There were 438 men authorized for an airborne division's engineering battalion. Of the three companies in the engineering battalion, two were parachute-qualified and the remaining company was not. Those not qualified as paratroopers wore the standard infantrymen's uniforms. In this picture we see soldiers with a mine detector, of which the airborne division engineering battalion had twenty authorized. (*National Archives*)

From the US Army Center of Military History collection is this wartime painting of CG-4A gliders prior to Operation NEPTUNE. The painting was done by Olin Dows. The canvas fabric that covered both the wings and fuselage of the CG-4A gliders was coated with a plasticized lacquer that provided it with a bit of rigidity and toughness, making it both waterproof and airtight.
(US Army Center for Military History)

In this picture of William C. Lee, considered 'the father of US Army airborne forces' for his tireless efforts in successfully promoting the concept to his superiors, he is wearing the two stars of a major general while in command of the 101st. He also played an important part in the planning for Operation NEPTUNE. On his chest are pewter 'jump wings' designed by a young army officer and approved for wear in March 1941. (National Archives)

In this picture we see a restored and operational example of the C-47 Skytrain in the Operation NEPTUNE recognition markings, which consisted of three broad white stripes interspaced with two black stripes on the aircraft's fuselage and wings. Despite the difficult job faced by pilots of the Troop Carrier Command, the organization did not receive priority for the best pilots. Rather, it was generally reserved for pilots that had failed to complete four-engine bomber training. (*DOD*)

In this image we see a C-47 Skytrain taking off with a CG-4A glider in tow. The glider was intended to be towed at a speed of approximately 152mph. When released from its tow cable, the descent speed was around 72mph. The gliders would stall at speeds under 70mph as they descended. Early-production CG-4As had wheels that were jettisoned following take-off. Later-production examples had the wheels permanently attached. (*National Archives*)

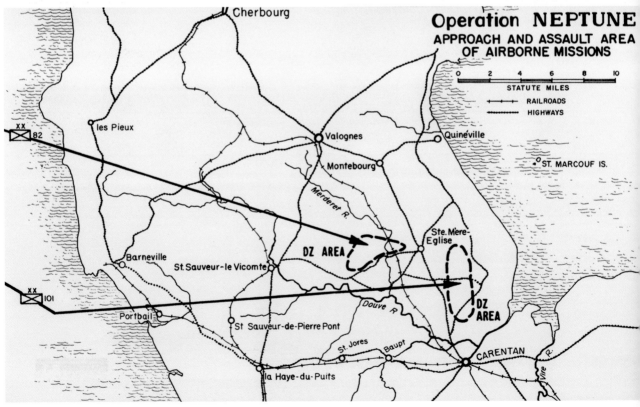

Operation NEPTUNE
APPROACH AND ASSAULT AREA
OF AIRBORNE MISSIONS

Cherbourg

0   2   4   6   8   10
STATUTE MILES
╫╫╫ RAILROADS
━━━ HIGHWAYS

les Pieux

XX 82

Valognes

Quineville

Montebourg

ST. MARCOUF IS.

Merderet R.

Ste. Mère-Eglise

DZ AREA

Barneville

St. Sauveur-le Vicomte

XX 101

Douve R.

DZ AREA

Portbail

St. Sauveur-de-Pierre Pont

St. Jores

Baupt

CARENTAN

Vire R.

la Haye-du-Puits

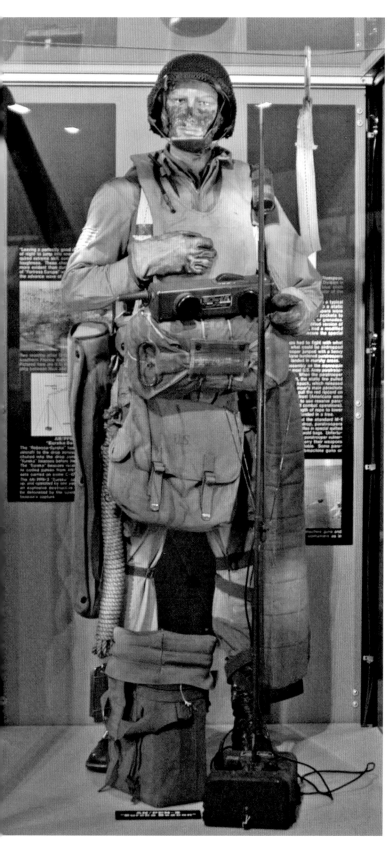

(**Opposite, above**) Detail of the tow-rope attachment point of a CG-4A glider. Also visible is a small portion of the standard 350ft-long nylon tow cable, with attached telephone cable, that allowed the glider pilots to remain in communication with the towing aircraft. US Army policy called for glider pilots to be immediately evacuated to the rear as soon as they completed their missions. They received no weapons training but were provided with pistols for self-defence. (*National Archives*)

(**Opposite, below**) The paratroopers of the 101st and 82nd were dropped near Sainte-Mère-Église and Carentan in Normandy, France during Operation NEPTUNE. Their missions were to secure road junctions and beach exits via which the US Army VII Corps could move off the beaches and capture the French port of Cherbourg. Some of the airborne troops landed near their objectives; however, most were scattered over a wide area. (*USAF Museum*)

(**Left**) This mannequin wears the uniform and various pieces of equipment carried by the paratroopers of the 82nd and 101st for 'the drop' into France during Operation NEPTUNE. Strapped to the mannequin's lower left thigh area is a coiled rope to aid him when forced to climb out of a tree. On the top of the reserve chute is the SCR-536, known as the 'Handie-Talkie'. At the mannequin's feet is the antenna for a larger radio. (*USAF Museum*)

(**Opposite, above**) It was not difficult for the German military to predict where Allied paratroopers and glider infantry would land if Normandy, France, was the chosen location. The Germans therefore built anti-glider obstacles nicknamed *Rommelspargel* or 'Rommel's Asparagus', as well as flooding low-lying areas to deny them to Allied airborne forces. The German military also fielded a large number of self-propelled anti-aircraft vehicles as pictured here to deal with any airborne threat. (*National Archives*)

(**Above**) Among the enemy military formations encountered by American paratroopers of the 82nd and 101st in Normandy were their German paratrooper counterparts, a mortar team of which is pictured here. However, by this point in the war most had never undergone training as paratroopers. They still considered themselves an elite, as did the American paratroopers, and fought with great determination. (*National Archives*)

(**Opposite, below**) Re-enactors portraying American paratroopers have set up a small display diorama incorporating an air-cooled M1919A4 .30 calibre machine gun and an M1 Garand Rifle. Due to the size and weight of the M1919A4 it was air-dropped in two separate bundles, one containing the machine gun and the other the tripod. In the October 1942 airborne division TO&E there were approximately 3,000 M1 Garand Rifles authorized. (*Ian Wilcox*)

The number one threat to the GIRs of the 82nd and 101st during Operation NEPTUNE proved not to be German anti-aircraft fire. Rather, it was the inability of glider pilots, after being released from their tows, to successfully land at night on terrain that was unforgiving and unfamiliar. The combination often proved deadly, as seen in this photograph. A total of 463 glider-delivered personnel died in Operation NEPTUNE, along with 57 glider pilots. (*National Archives*)

The M1941 Parson field jacket, the canvas leggings and the lack of jump boots mark this soldier as a glider infantryman who has taken a defensive position behind a Normandy hedgerow. The great degree of resentment between the paratroopers and glider infantry centred around the latter not receiving any extra hazardous duty pay as the paratroopers did. This arrangement did not change until after Operation NEPTUNE. (*National Archives*)

In the standard twelve-man US Army infantry squad of the Second World War, there was a single Browning Automatic Rifle (BAR) as shown here. Due to the weapon's weight and the fact that it could not be broken down into easily transportable components, it was not considered safe for paratroopers to carry into combat. Therefore each paratrooper infantry squad had the air-cooled M1919A4 .30 calibre machine gun (and a spare) in its place. *(DOD)*

As the GIRs could bring in heavier weapons than those of the PIRs, the units' structure differed. Each GIR had the ability to bring fifteen units of the 0.25-ton truck, commonly known as the 'Jeep', to their landing zones. The private collector's Jeep pictured here is fitted with a dummy replica of the .50 calibre M2HB machine guns that would be employed by the GIR mobile heavy weapons company. *(Chris Hughes)*

The 1942 airborne division TO&E authorized thirty-six units of the M1 81mm Mortar pictured here. Depending on the type of round fired, the 81mm mortar had a maximum range of 3,290 yards. Each PIR had twenty-seven of the 81mm mortars, while every GIR was issued with twenty-four. The normal rate of fire was eighteen rounds per minute. (*National Archives*)

Designed specifically for airborne division use was the M3 105mm Howitzer pictured here. It first appeared in the airborne division inventory before Operation NEPTUNE to supplement the fire-power of the division's M1 75mm Howitzers. It was not officially authorized for airborne division employment until the December 1944 TO&E. (*Pierre-Olivier Buan*)

In this post-Second World War photograph, we see General Matthew B. Ridgway, commander of the 82nd in Sicily, Italy and France. He was made commander of the newly-formed XVIII Airborne Corps in August 1944. During the Korean War, he initially commanded the 8th Army until becoming commander of all American and United Nations forces in Korea. He would go on to become chief of staff of the US Army between 1953 and 1955. (*National Archives*)

Chapter Two

Late-War Action

The dramatic collapse of the German defensive lines in Normandy following Operation COBRA (25 to 31 July 1944) allowed the US First Army and the newly-formed Third Army to advance towards Paris and beyond at a much faster pace than initially envisioned. This resulted in the cancellation of many proposed airborne operations as the anticipated objectives fell to the advancing Allied ground forces, which included British and Commonwealth units, ahead of schedule.

Logistical shortfalls beginning in late August 1944 would eventually bring the fast-paced Allied advance through France and towards Germany to a gradual halt. To bring the war in the ETO to an end by Christmas 1944, in early September 1944 British Field Marshal Bernard Law Montgomery proposed a bold plan for a combined airborne and ground assault to seize and hold half a dozen bridges in German-occupied Holland and the single highway that connected them all.

If the airborne portion of Montgomery's proposed assault was a success, the armoured and infantry divisions of the British Army XXX Corps could use the highway and the captured bridges to plunge deep behind enemy lines and then advance into the Ruhr, the industrial heartland of Germany. This would hopefully bring the war in Europe to an end by Christmas of 1944.

The US Army Contribution

Eisenhower, Montgomery's superior, was in full support of the proposed combined airborne and ground assault into Holland and approved it on 10 September 1944. He had in mid-July 1944 asked his staff to prepare for an airborne plan that would, in his words, be marked by 'imagination and daring'. Eisenhower's superior, Marshall, as well as General Henry H. Arnold, the commanding general of the USAAF, also wanted to see what a large-scale airborne assault was capable of achieving in the ETO.

Not wanting a repeat of what had happened following Operation NEPTUNE, with the US Army's two airborne divisions retained on the front lines for more than a month, before assigning the 82nd and 101st to Montgomery's command, Eisenhower had stipulated that they be pulled from front-line duty as soon as British Army ground troops reached and passed the positions. Eisenhower and other senior US Army officers wanted to maintain the 82nd and 101st in 'theatre reserve' so they could take quick advantage of any opportunities that might arise that would be suitable for large-scale airborne operations.

The Airborne Forces Assigned

The code-name assigned to Montgomery's plan for the capture of the six bridges in German-occupied Holland was Operation MARKET GARDEN. The airborne portion was labelled Operation MARKET and the ground portion Operation GARDEN. For Operation MARKET the 82nd and the 101st were transferred from the US Army XVIII Airborne Corps to the British 1st Airborne Corps, which was already in command of the 1st British Airborne Division.

The US Army's 17th Airborne Division, of which the leading elements arrived in England on 26 August 1944, was not assigned to Operation MARKET as it still lacked all of its authorized equipment.

The 1st British Airborne Division's objective for Operation MARKET was the large highway bridge located at the Dutch town of Arnhem, approximately 60 miles behind German lines. The US Army's 82nd and 101st were assigned a much larger variety of objectives behind German lines in Holland, which included bridges, large and small along the single highway that led to the bridge at Arnhem, as well as a key terrain feature along the same route. If all went to plan, a British armoured division of the XXX Corps, which comprised part of Operation GARDEN, was anticipated to reach Arnhem by day four or five of the offensive.

Lessons Learned are Applied

Rather than having a large number of spread-out drop and landing zones for the two US Army airborne divisions as had been put into place for Operation NEPTUNE, Operation MARKET would take place in daylight and there would be far fewer drop and landing zones. All of this was intended to make it easier for the pilots of the Troop Carrier Command to locate them.

The switch to a daylight operation came about for a couple of reasons. First, there were the poor results achieved with the prior nighttime operations. In addition, there would be a lack of any moonlight on the date chosen to begin Operation MARKET.

There was another advantage in having fewer drop and landing zones for Operation MARKET. The paratroopers and glider infantry of the 82nd and 101st could, in theory, quickly marshal themselves in sufficient numbers before marching on to their assigned objectives, something that proved very difficult during Operation NEPTUNE and led to the failure of important parts of the endeavour.

The Opening Act

Beginning 17 September 1944, the US Army's participation in Operation MARKET began. Plans called for the 82nd and 101st to be transported to their objectives over a four-day period, concluding on 20 September. The 82nd would be delivered by 400 transport aircraft and 209 gliders, and the 101st by 428 transport aircraft and 70 gliders.

The objectives assigned to the 82nd for Operation MARKET were closer to Arnhem than those of the 101st. Those of the 101st were nearer to the British Army's front-line positions along the Dutch-Belgian border. Both the 82nd and 101st went into Operation MARKET with three PIRs and a single GIR.

Let Us Try Something Different

With fewer drop and landing zones, the Troop Carrier Command pilots, aided by pathfinders placed into position twenty minutes earlier, maintained extremely tight serials and deposited the bulk of the 82nd and 101st either directly on their chosen locations or very close by. Losses of transport aircraft and gliders compared to Operation NEPTUNE proved low, as Allied fighters and bombers effectively suppressed most of the German anti-aircraft defences before the airlift began.

The commanders of both US Army airborne divisions would have preferred having the bulk of their forces delivered on the first day of Operation MARKET. However, a shortage of transport aircraft and the distance between the airfields located in England from which the transport planes flew made that impossible to implement. Unfortunately, airfields closer to the objectives on the European continent that would have allowed the transport aircraft to make more than one airlift per day remained crowded with Allied fighters and other shorter-range tactical aircraft.

Operation MARKET GARDEN Unfolds

The inability to land a sufficient number of US Army paratroopers and glider infantry on the first day of Operation MARKET resulted in some of the assigned objectives not being seized per the very tight and what proved to be unrealistic timetable.

Compounding the woes of all three Allied airborne divisions participating in Operation MARKET, the optimum weather conditions present on 17 September were replaced by much less favourable conditions for the next few days, leading to serious delays in delivering additional men and equipment. These led in turn to other delays, and as German resistance became progressively stronger day by day, the Operation MARKET GARDEN timetable quickly began to unravel.

From the regimental after-action report of the 502nd PIR comes this extract describing how German resistance quickly intensified:

Action began at 0520, on the 18th of September, when the enemy opened fire with automatic fire on the battalion's positions on the front and left flank. It became heavier through the day, with artillery and mortar fire supporting the fire of the small arms and 20mm AA [anti-aircraft] gunfire. This heavy fire kept up throughout the day, with the enemy seeming to fire in an area rather than at separate targets. In the morning, the enemy made two determined attacks supported by heavy artillery and mortar concentrations. These were repulsed with heavy losses to the enemy. However, during the morning, many casualties were caused by infiltrating enemy, and the heavy concentration of fire poured into the pine growths in which the battalion had taken up position. Support weapons of the battalion were limited to two 81mm mortars and five 60mm mortars. Supply lines were long and hazardous, and vehicles were not available.

On the evening of 18 September, a British armoured division of the XXX Corps reached the 101st sector as planned. The next morning advance elements of the same British armoured division reached the 82nd sector. Unfortunately, two key bridges in the Dutch city of Nijmegen, one a railroad bridge and the other a highway bridge, which would have allowed the British armoured division to drive for another 10 miles to reach Arnhem, had not been captured by the 82nd as planned on 17 September or on the following morning.

The efforts made by the men of the 101st in trying to capture the Dutch bridges appear in this extract from the Medal of Honor Citation of Private First-Class Joe E. Mann:

> He distinguished himself by conspicuous gallantry above and beyond the call of duty. On 18 September 1944, in the vicinity of Best [sic], Holland, his platoon, attempting to seize the bridge across the Wilhelmina Canal, was surrounded and isolated by an enemy force greatly superior in personnel and firepower. Acting as lead scout, Pfc. Mann boldly crept to within rocket-launcher range of an enemy artillery position and, in the face of heavy enemy fire, destroyed an 88mm gun and an ammunition dump. Completely disregarding the great danger involved, he remained in his exposed position, and, with his M-1 rifle, killed the enemy one by one until he was wounded four times.

The failure of the 82nd to secure either the railroad or highway bridge at Nijmegen on schedule came about due to the lack of sufficient manpower available to one-star Brigadier General James M. Gavin, commander of the division, who had replaced Ridgway. Gavin was promoted to major general in October 1944, the rank required to command a division.

Gavin had been forced to divide his existing strength between the seizure of an area of high ground near the bridges, accomplished as planned on 17 September, but this had not left him sufficient manpower to take the railroad or highway bridges. The high ground secured was to act as a blocking position in case of German counter-attacks from a nearby forest that had been reported by the Dutch underground to contain an enemy armoured formation and deny the area to German artillery observers.

A Dismal Ending

Even with the support of the arriving British armoured division, the railroad and highway bridge at Nijmegen remained unsecured until the early evening of the 20th. An important element of the operation that finally secured those bridges involved a paratrooper battalion from the 82nd crossing the Waal River, to the west of the railroad bridge, in British Army-supplied assault boats, on the afternoon of the 20th. Despite taking heavy casualties, they disrupted the German defenders badly enough to allow the British tanks to first cross and hold the railroad bridge and then go on and capture the highway bridge.

The next day the British tankers set out for the bridge at Arnhem, but it was already too late as the last of the British paratroopers near the bridge had been routed by strong German counter-attacks.

The official ending of Operation MARKET GARDEN took place on 25 September when the surviving British 1st Airborne Division personnel behind German lines were ordered to withdraw to the safety of Allied front-line positions. British losses killed, wounded and missing during Operation MARKET GARDEN were 7,212 men. The 82nd lost 1,423 and the 101st 2,110. If all the Allied military personnel involved in Operation MARKET GARDEN are included, including pilots and flight-crews, the total casualties are approximately 12,000 men.

The ruins of the bridge at Arnhem, which had been the main objective of MARKET GARDEN, were not captured by the British Army until April 1945. It had been destroyed by USAAF bombers on 7 October 1944 to prevent use by the Germans.

The Fighting Goes On

Unfortunately for the 82nd and 101st, the official end of Operation MARKET GARDEN did not result in their relief as Eisenhower had stipulated to Montgomery

---

Operation MARKET GARDEN in Film

The long list of all the things that went wrong with Operation MARKET GARDEN appeared in the 1977 film titled *A Bridge Too Far*. The movie's plotline came from a book of the same name by British wartime journalist Cornelius Ryan. The primary focus of the film is the British 1st Airborne Division's attempt to seize the bridge at Arnhem and their efforts to hold on to it despite German counter-attacks.

Not ignored but playing a smaller role in the movie are the US Army airborne division efforts to secure the road and bridges leading to Arnhem. As was typical of American-British movie co-productions of the day, there were a great many cameo appearances in the film of the leading male actors from both countries. The British side included Sean Connery and Michael Caine and from the American side came James Caan, Elliott Gould, Gene Hackman and Robert Redford.

before the airborne operation took place. Rather, the British and Commonwealth forces under Montgomery, like the US Army, were short of infantry divisions. So the US Army's two airborne divisions, with British Army support, remained in the salient created by Operation MARKET GARDEN.

Brereton, the commander of the FAAA, wrote to Eisenhower on 10 October 1944: 'Keeping airborne soldiers in the front lines as infantry is a violation of the cardinal rules of airborne employment.' In protesting their continued use, Brereton stated that unless the airborne divisions could withdraw immediately, he could not meet a ready date for a proposed airborne operation to assist the 12th Army Group under Bradley's command. 'Further combat,' he warned, 'will deplete them of trained men beyond replacement capacity.'

Despite Brereton's concerns, the two US Army airborne divisions remained on the front lines going into November 1944. The 82nd was finally relieved on 11 November 1944 and the 101st on 20 November 1944. Despite German counter-attacks tapering off by the end of October 1944, between 26 September and 20 November 1944, the two airborne divisions had combined losses of approximately 4,000 men.

Modifying the TO&E

Instead of returning to England for rest and refit as had occurred following Operation NEPTUNE, the 82nd and the 101st withdrew to the rear areas in Allied-occupied France and went into theatre reserve. The 17th Airborne Division remained in England for the time being. All three divisions were under the oversight of the XVIII Airborne Corps.

It had become apparent that despite airborne doctrine, the quick withdrawal of the US Army's airborne division following a large-scale operation was not working out in practice. The February 1944 airborne division TO&E, therefore, was slightly modified in August 1944.

The August 1944 airborne division TO&E, compared to the February 1944 airborne division TO&E, included more weaponry, a parachute maintenance company and 34 trucks more than the 425 in the February airborne division TO&E. The authorized manpower for the airborne divisions' TO&Es (October 1942, February 1944 and August 1944) remained at just under 9,000 men.

Off to the Pacific

The 11th Airborne Division remained in the United States as a reserve force until January 1944, when it was shipped overseas with its first elements arriving in New Guinea in late May 1944. Interestingly enough, the 11th would be the only US Army airborne division of the Second World War that would retain the original October 1942 TO&E, which called for a single PIR and two GIRs.

After a period of intense training and acclimatization in New Guinea, the 11th was committed to combat on the Philippine island of Leyte in November 1944, performing the role of an infantry division. It continued in that role when moved to the Philippine island of Luzon in January 1944, where it remained until the war's end.

As the ETO had priority for transport aircraft and gliders, the 11th Airborne Division was never able to conduct a division-sized airborne operation. On three occasions it did conduct successful smaller airborne operations – in December 1944, February 1945 and June 1945 – ranging from company to regiment-sized.

The best-known airborne operation conducted by the 11th during the Second World War was dramatized in *The Great Raid*, a 2005 movie starring American actors Benjamin Bratt and James Franco. The story centred on the division's attempt in June 1945 to free prisoners of war held at Cabanatuan prison camp in the Philippines.

Into the Breach Once Again

In the early-morning hours of 16 December 1944, Hitler launched a massive counter-offensive operation code-named *Wacht am Rhein* (Watch on the Rhine) of approximately thirty divisions against four divisions of the American First Army that were holding defensive lines in the Ardennes Forest of Belgium and Luxembourg.

The German counter-offensive would last until 28 January 1945, with the series of engagements that it comprised commonly referred to as the 'Battle of the Bulge'. At its high point, the German crescent-shaped 'bulge' was 60 miles deep by 80 miles wide behind American lines.

To help stem the time-sensitive German advance, the XVIII Airborne Corps with two of its divisions, the 82nd and 101st, was transferred to Bradley's 12th Army Group on 17 December 1944. Still refitting after the hard fighting in Holland, neither airborne division had regained what the US Army considered a fully operational status, something not expected to be completed until January 1945.

The 17th Airborne Division was ordered from England to France as quickly as possible, but due to poor weather conditions it was not ready for action until 24 December 1944. The following day the division was transferred to Patton's Third Army. It saw its first combat on 3 January 1945 and remained under the control of Third Army until 10 February 1945, when it was relieved and placed back into theatre reserve as part of the XVIII Airborne Corps.

The Assignments

The 101st received the job of holding the Belgian town of Bastogne with three PIRs, along with a mix of other units composed of surviving elements of those US Army divisions that had been forced to retreat in the face of the initial German attacks.

The 101st arrived in Bastogne after an eight-hour 107-mile trip in the darkness, on the evening of 19 December. Bastogne was a road junction and, if held, would deny the Germans mobility as well as a choke point to slow the German offensive. If successful, it would allow time for the US Army in the ETO to reorient and reorganize itself to counter-attack the flanks of the German advance.

It was the 10th Armored Division that delayed the attacking German divisions long enough for the 101st to reach and secure Bastogne. Elements of the division then became part of the forces defending Bastogne.

As the two PIRs and the single GIR of the 82nd left for Belgium before the 101st, the decision came through that it would pass through Bastogne and deploy to its north at the town of Werbomont. From this location, it could aid in defending the northern shoulder of the bulge. The 82nd arrived in Werbomont on 18 December and the next morning began to spread into the surrounding areas to establish a defensive screen around the town.

Marino M. Michetti of the 508th PIR, 82nd Airborne Division, remembers what occurred in mid-December 1944 when his division found itself ordered to Belgium:

> That night we spent in packing personal belongings, drawing weapons from supply, and getting set for our move in the morning. By 0900 on December 18, the 508th, loaded in huge tractor-trailer trucks (Red Ball Express), joined the division convoy as it left Sissonne, France, and headed for Werbomont, a small village in Belgium. At 1800 on December 19, twelve hours after the regiment arrived at Werbomont, we got orders to move up to Chevron, two miles east. We made this move on foot … Marching on the snow-covered road, we met soldiers and tanks moving to the rear. I did not know where we were going except to meet the Germans where these other soldiers had run into a hell of a lot of them.

The Fighting

Under intense pressure from three German Waffen SS armoured divisions, the 82nd was ordered to withdraw from its original defensive lines around Werbomont on 24 December by higher command. It quickly re-established new defensive lines the following day, which the Waffen SS armoured divisions failed to outflank or penetrate. The bulk of the three enemy armoured divisions transferred to another sector on 28 December.

To keep up the pressure on the 82nd, elements of the Waffen SS armoured divisions stayed, and with the assistance of a German infantry division, continued to attack without success. A member of the 82nd, Allan H. Stein, recalls his thoughts on the fighting around the Werbomont area:

> On the 24th [December 1944] we dug into a field. That night, what seemed like an entire German battalion hit our positions. Our entire line opened up in continuous fire until we were down to a few clips. Cans of loose ammo were

brought to us to reload our clips. At that time, I thought it was the proper moment to try my bazooka. I aimed it at where our outpost had been. I fired it, and 'Bam' it hit a tree ... It was discovered that my tree burst had broken up a platoon of Germans getting ready to hit our position. Their bodies were punctured by wood and shrapnel.

By 3 January 1945, the German counter-offensive had run out of steam, and the 82nd went on the offensive with the assistance of other units. An example of the fierce fighting by the men of the division appears in this extract from the Medal of Honor citation for First Sergeant Leonard A. Funk for an action on 29 January 1945:

> ... under his skillful and courageous leadership, this miscellaneous group and the 3rd Platoon attacked fifteen houses, cleared them, and took thirty prisoners without suffering a casualty. The fierce drive of Company C quickly overran Holzheim, netting some eighty prisoners, who were placed under a four-man guard, all that could be spared, while the rest of the understrength unit went about mopping up isolated points of resistance. An enemy patrol, by means of a ruse, succeeded in capturing the guards and freeing the prisoners and had begun preparations to attack Company C from the rear when 1st Sgt. Funk walked around the building and into their midst. He was ordered to surrender by a German officer who pushed a machine pistol into his stomach. Although over-whelmingly outnumbered and facing almost certain death, 1st Sgt. Funk, pre-tending to comply with the order, began slowly to unsling his submachine gun from his shoulder and then, with lightning motion, brought the muzzle into line and riddled the German officer. He turned upon the other Germans, firing and shouting to the other Americans to seize the enemy's weapons. In the ensuing fight, twenty-one Germans were killed, many wounded, and the remainder captured. 1st Sgt. Funk's bold action and heroic disregard for his own safety were directly responsible for the recapture of a vastly superior enemy force, which, if allowed to remain free, could have taken the widespread units of Company C by surprise and endangered the entire attack plan.

The 82nd found itself pulled from the front lines in Belgium on 6 February 1945. The division's casualties came in at about 5,000 men.

The Battle for Bastogne

One of the best-known incidents during the siege of Bastogne took place on the evening of 21 December 1944. The Germans had surrounded the town the day before, sending emissaries with a note to the commander of Bastogne, in this case Brigadier General Anthony C. McAuliffe of the 101st, to surrender all the forces defending the town in two hours. McAuliffe expressed his contempt for the German

The Siege of Bastogne in Film

A 1949 Hollywood-made film titled *Battleground* is a fictionalized account of the experiences of a company of glider infantrymen from the 101st during the siege of Bastogne. Despite being fictionalized, some of the scenes in the movie were based on events that took place during the fighting.

An officer from the 101st that fought at Bastogne was the technical advisor to the film. Twenty veterans of the 101st that also served at Bastogne were brought in to train the actors in how to realistically portray US Army soldiers; they would also go on to serve as extras during the filming. Some well-known American actors that starred in the film included Van Johnson, James Whitmore and Ricardo Montalban.

surrender demand with his famous reply 'Nuts', delivered to the German emissaries who had brought the surrender demand the previous day. When the Germans proved puzzled by the term, an American officer present was kind enough to explain to the Germans that it meant 'Go to Hell.'

Robert M. Brown of the 101st recorded vivid reminiscences about the fierce fighting around Bastogne, and his capture by the Germans appears in this passage:

> ... my company was manning roadblocks on the western perimeter of the encircled city [Bastogne] near Flamierge. We had repulsed attacks in our sector on the 19th, 20th, and 22nd. On the 23rd the Germans came again early in the morning out of a heavy fog which hung over the bitter-cold, snow-covered hills, wearing snowsuits and with tanks painted white ... There was little support from division artillery because of an ammunition shortage, but our 81mm mortars were a big help ... I was wounded about 1600 and put in a basement of a house just behind the main line of resistance where the medics had set up an aid station. The roadblock fell just after dark. All the wounded and medics, the crews of the armor, and a few men from Company C were captured, all that remained of the reinforced platoon that held the position.

The German siege of Bastogne was partially lifted in the afternoon of 26 December 1944 by the leading elements of the 4th Armored Division belonging to Lieutenant General George S. Patton's Third Army. There remained weeks of hard fighting ahead of the 101st until finally relieved on 26 January 1945. Casualties suffered by the division totalled approximately 2,500 men.

Another TO&E Reorganization

The August 1944 airborne division officially-authorized TO&E found itself replaced in December 1944 by a new TO&E done with Marshall's full support. He had long felt that AGF leadership (McNair was killed in a friendly-fire incident the previous month) needed to pay more attention to what the airborne division commanders believed was necessary for success on and off the battlefield. In the logistical support role, the December 1944 TO&E for airborne divisions called for 1,028 trucks.

The unofficial two PIRs and single GIR TO&E structure of the 82nd in place for Operation HUSKY in July 1943 and during the Battle of the Bulge, December 1944 through to January 1945, was finally formalized with the December 1944 airborne division TO&E. It also authorized the addition of a third battalion to the division's GIR, which had been unofficial policy anyway for both the 82nd and 101st since before Operation NEPTUNE.

Authorized airborne division manpower with the December 1944 TO&E rose to around 13,000 men. US Army infantry divisions at that time had approximately 14,000 men, and armoured divisions had 11,000 men. The actual reorganization of the airborne divisions to the last wartime TO&E change took place between February and March 1945.

The Last Airborne Operation

In early November 1944, Eisenhower's staff began preparing plans for an airborne operation over the River Rhine into Germany, on the premise that the various Allied armies had reached the river by that time. However, the unexpected Battle of the Bulge brought an end to any such plans.

When Montgomery's forces finally reached the Rhine in early 1945, plans for a combined ground-airborne operation over the Rhine began to coalesce once again into what became known as Operation PLUNGER. The airborne portion, referred to as Operation VARSITY, came under the command of the XVIII Airborne Corps.

The heavy toll imposed on the men and equipment of the 82nd and 101st by the fighting during the Battle of the Bulge meant that neither airborne division proved ready for participation in Operation VARSITY, leaving the XVIII Airborne Corps with just three combat-ready airborne divisions: the newly-arrived US Army 13th Airborne Division, the US Army 17th Airborne Division and the British Army 6th Airborne Division.

Let Us Try Something Different

Based on what had occurred during Operation MARKET in September 1944, a much-debated decision came about that for Operation VARSITY almost the entire assets of the airborne divisions assigned were to be brought to their objectives in a single airlift, within a span of about four hours. The dilemma for the XVIII Airborne Corps was that they only had enough transport aircraft on hand to deliver two airborne divisions at a time. As a result, the decision came about to employ only the US Army 17th Airborne Division and the British Army 6th Airborne Division.

Airborne Tanks

During the early part of the Second World War, the US Army had become enthusiastic about the prospect of forming airborne tank battalions flown into enemy airfields that had been captured by PIRs or GIRs. This resulted in the creation of an airborne tank company, and later an airborne tank battalion, both in 1943. Unfortunately, the successful fielding of these units revolved around having both a suitable light tank and a large enough aircraft or glider that could deliver it to the battlefield.

The airborne tank turned out to be the three-man M22 Light Tank. As there was no glider in the US Army inventory that was large enough to hold it, the plans called for it to be conveyed to its objective by the USAAF four-engine 'C-54 Skymaster'. Due to the M22's size it was too large to fit within the plane's fuselage, therefore the tank's turret was to be secured within the C-54's fuselage and the hull under the fuselage. The two components were to be mated after landing at a captured enemy airfield.

Because the M22 proved to be both under-gunned and under-armoured, the US Army soon lost interest in the idea of airborne tanks. The single airborne tank company equipped with the M22 was never shipped overseas, and the single airborne tank battalion equipped with the M22 found itself converted into a medium tank battalion in October 1944. The majority of the 822 units of the M22 constructed between April 1943 and February 1944 were placed immediately into storage until most were scrapped post-war.

In another change to accepted airborne doctrine, the ground portion of Operation PLUNGER, beginning on the evening of 23 March 1945, would start before its airborne component, Operation VARSITY. Also, the two airborne divisions' objectives were all to be within range of Allied artillery. The US Army 17th Airborne Division arrived on its objectives on the morning of 24 March 1945, aboard 903 transport planes and 897 gliders. The aircraft of the Troop Carrier Command flew in from airfields in France.

Rather than having the airborne forces of Operation VARSITY land in areas away from enemy ground forces and anti-aircraft emplacements, this time they were dropped closer than ever before so that they could smother enemy resistance when they reached the ground. This appears in the Medal of Honor citation of Private First-Class George J. Peters of the 17th Airborne Division:

Private Peters, a platoon radio operator with Company G, made a descent into Germany near Fluren, east of the Rhine. With ten others, he landed in a field about 75 yards from a German machine-gun supported by riflemen and was immediately pinned down by heavy, direct fire. The position of the small unit seemed hopeless with men struggling to free themselves of their parachutes in a hail of bullets that cut them off from their nearby equipment bundles when Pvt. Peters stood up without orders and began a one-man charge against the hostile emplacement armed only with a rifle and grenades. His single-handed assault immediately drew the enemy fire away from his comrades. He had run halfway to his objective, pitting rifle fire against that of the machine gun, when he was struck and knocked to the ground by a burst. Heroically, he regained his feet and struggled onward. Once more he was torn by bullets, and this time he was unable to rise. With gallant devotion to his self-imposed mission, he crawled directly into the fire that had mortally wounded him until close enough to hurl grenades which knocked out the machine-gun, killed two of its operators, and drove protecting riflemen from their positions into the safety of a woods. By his intrepidity and supreme sacrifice, Pvt. Peters saved the lives of many of his fellow soldiers and made it possible for them to reach their equipment, organize, and seize their first objective.

German resistance to the 17th Airborne Division's part in Operation VARSITY varied, with some units facing stiff enemy resistance and others far less so. By the early afternoon of 24 March 1945, all objectives assigned to the 17th Airborne Division had been secured. Remaining German opposition in the surrounding areas collapsed by 27 March 1945, and a British Army armoured brigade entered into the sector held by the American airborne division.

Total American casualties through 27 March were 1,584. On 29 March 1945, the US Army Second Armored Division passed through the 17th Airborne Division sector to link up with the 3rd Armored Division in securing the Ruhr, the industrial heartland of Germany.

Proposed Late-War Airborne Operations

There were some additional airborne operations proposed between March and April 1945. One of the most ambitious was seizing an airport near the German capital of Berlin and securing the city if there was a relatively rapid collapse of the existing government. It would involve at least three airborne divisions of the XVIII Airborne Corps and be assigned the code-name Operation ECLIPSE.

Another late-war airborne operation considered was code-named Operation JUBILANT and revolved around seizing some German prisoner-of-war camps lest the Germans guarding them should attempt to harm the American military personnel held within. None of these airborne operations came to fruition as events on the ground and the disintegration of the German military led to them being unnecessary.

The necessity of Operation VARSITY was questioned post-war by historian Charles B. MacDonald in the official US Army Center for Military History publication titled *The Last Offensive*, as seen in the following passage:

Although the objectives assigned the [airborne] divisions were legitimate, they were objectives the ground troops alone under existing circumstances should have been able to take without undue difficulty and probably with considerably fewer casualties. Participation by paratroopers and glidermen gave appreciably no more depth to the bridgehead at Wesel [Germany] than that achieved by infantrymen of the 30th Division.

Getting to the End

Despite not being considered combat-ready for Operation VARSITY, the 82nd and the 101st were both pushed into front-line service for the remainder of the war. The 101st went to the Seventh Army located in southern Germany and the 82nd remained with the XVIII Airborne Corps. From a small booklet published by the *Stars and Stripes* military newspaper appears this passage regarding the final contribution to the war in the ETO by the 82nd:

On the move again, All-Americans guarded the west bank of the Rhine in the Cologne area in early April [1945]; Co. A 504th was awarded the Presidential Citation for a daring raid across the river. While most of the division still was entrained, the 505th stormed across the Elbe River, April 30 [1945]. Other outfits hurled themselves into the battle as fast as they arrived. The German Twenty-first Army, with an estimated strength of 144,000, surrendered to the 82nd at Ludwigslust [Germany], about 25 miles east of the Elbe [River], May 3 [1945]. Next day, 25 miles east, patrol contact was made with Soviet troops.

Their Fate

The official German surrender occurred on 7 May 1945. In comparatively short order the existing command structure of the airborne divisions in the ETO began to change. The FAAA was deactivated on 20 May 1945.

The XVIII Airborne Corps was in transit from the ETO to the Pacific to prepare for the invasion of Japan, code-named Operation DOWNFALL. However, with the formal Japanese surrender on 2 September 1945, the XVIII Airborne Corps was rendered redundant and eventually deactivated on 15 October 1945.

The various US Army airborne divisions raised during the Second World War suffered different fates. The 17th Airborne Division deactivated on 15 September 1945 and the 101st on 30 November 1945. On 25 February 1946, the 13th Airborne Division received orders to deactivate. Both the 11th and 82nd Airborne divisions found themselves retained in the immediate aftermath of the Second World War.

The Supreme Commander Allied Expeditionary Force Dwight D. Eisenhower oversaw the land battle strategy of the Western Allied armies in the ETO. General Bernard Law Montgomery was commander of all Western Allied ground forces in the ETO until 1 September 1944 when Eisenhower also took over that role. This had been agreed upon by the Western Allies before the invasion of the Continent. (*National Archives*)

Between June and September 1944, German losses numbered in the hundreds of thousands; killed, wounded or captured as seen here. It was these numbers that convinced Eisenhower and Montgomery in early September 1944 that the German Army was near collapse and that a bold offensive on a narrow front into German-occupied Holland might end the war by Christmas 1944. (*National Archives*)

(**Opposite, above**) The plan to end the war in the ETO, conceived in early September 1944, was code-named Operation MARKET GARDEN. The airborne division portion of that endeavour received the label Operation MARKET. Spearheading that operation was the British Army 1st Airborne Division, tasked with the capture of the highway bridge spanning the River Rhine at Arnhem in the Netherlands. Pictured are re-enactors wearing the Second World War uniforms like those of the British paratroopers. (*Christophe Vallier*)

(**Opposite, below**) The ground portion of Operation MARKET GARDEN was named Operation GARDEN and spearheaded by the Guards Armoured Division of the British XXX Corps. It was to reach the bridge at Arnhem, secured by the British Army 1st Airborne Division, within forty-eight hours. Leading the Guards Armoured Division to Arnhem was its divisional reconnaissance element, employing various types of armoured cars such as the Humber Mark III seen here. (*Ian Wilcox*)

(**Above**) Despite Eisenhower and Montgomery being convinced of the near total collapse of the German Army in early September 1944, the situation had dramatically changed by the middle of September 1944. By that time, the German Army had begun to stabilize its front lines and bring up reinforcements, following the long retreat from the disastrous encirclement and heavy losses in the Falaise Pocket. Pictured here is a German Army officer briefing one of his men. (*National Archives*)

(**Opposite, above**) In the short period before Operation MARKET GARDEN began, there was a growing awareness among many in both the British and American armies that the German armed forces had dramatically increased the number of troops and tanks in the areas intended to be seized by the American and British paratroopers. The concerns raised by this situation were ignored by Montgomery, with fatal consequences for the British 1st Airborne Corps. Pictured is a late-model production Panzer IV. (*Pierre-Olivier Buan*)

(**Opposite, below**) In this photograph, we see Brigadier General James M. Gavin, commander of the 82nd, briefing his senior officers on the upcoming Operation MARKET. He and the majority of his fellow officers are wearing a modified version of the dark green, post-Operation NEPTUNE two-piece 1943 standard army field uniforms. The paratrooper version had cargo pockets on the pants with tie-down straps, which the standard infantrymen's pants lacked. (*National Archives*)

(**Above**) Post-Operation NEPTUNE, 82nd Division armourers are maintaining an assortment of weapons. The two soldiers on the right-hand side of the photograph are glider infantrymen as indicated by the circular glider patches on their garrison caps. A pewter glider badge, similar in appearance to the paratrooper's badge but with a forward view of a glider rather than an open parachute, was authorized following Operation NEPTUNE. (*National Archives*)

(**Above**) US Army paratroopers are shown heading towards their assigned C-47 Skytrain. Once on their aircraft, they were referred to as a 'stick', which could comprise anywhere between fifteen and eighteen men. When over their assigned drop zone, the first out of the transport plane was supposed to be an officer, if present. If no officers were on board, then a senior non-commissioned officer (NCO) would be the first out, with the last man out being a junior NCO. (*National Archives*)

(**Opposite, above**) For some of the larger and heavier equipment required by paratroopers upon landing, the US Army employed the Type A-5 Aerial Delivery Container commonly referred to as the 'Para-Pac'. It would be attached to the bottom fuselage of the C-47 Skytrain as pictured here and released at the same time that the paratroopers exited their planes. It was 56in in length and 15in in diameter and made of canvas and web fabric. (*National Archives*)

(**Opposite, below**) Pictured here are CG-4A gliders lined up for Operation MARKET. The rifle squads of the GIRs were composed of twelve men. Each GIR rifle squad consisted of a senior NCO as the squad leader, assisted by a junior NCO acting as the assistant squad leader. Up until the December 1944 airborne division TO&E, the only weapon officially authorized for the GIR rifle squad was the M1 Garand Rifle. With the December 1944 TO&E, each GIR rifle squad was authorized a single Browning Automatic Rifle (BAR). (*National Archives*)

195169

(**Opposite, above**) Visible on the nose of the CG-4A glider being loaded with a 0.25-ton truck (Jeep) is a device known as the Ludington-Griswold nose modification. It was constructed of welded steel pipes and intended to strengthen the otherwise fragile cockpit to protect the glider pilots and passengers against obstacles while landing. It appeared on some CG-4A gliders before Operation NEPTUNE. (*National Archives*)

(**Opposite, below**) Major General Maxwell Taylor, the commander of the 101st, is seen here providing a salute to the photographer, having just boarded his transport aircraft for Operation MARKET. The shiny circular metal object located just above his reserve chute is a single-point quick-release buckle. It marks his parachute as being the new T-7. The previous T-5 parachute lacked a quick-release buckle, requiring a paratrooper to unfasten three snap hooks before he could remove his parachutes and harness; a difficult task, let alone under fire. (*National Archives*)

(**Above**) In a photograph taken on 17 September 1944, just before Operation MARKET, we see the interior of the C-47 Skytrain assigned to carry Brigadier General James M. Gavin, commander of the 82nd, and his command staff into combat. The August 1944 airborne division TO&E called for a total of 563 officers. They were authorized both pistols and M1 Carbines, although many, including Gavin, preferred the M1 Garand Rifle. (*National Archives*)

(**Above**) As the flight path for Allied bombers heading towards German industry in the Ruhr Valley passed over Holland, there was a large concentration of German anti-aircraft guns of various types and sizes, including the 8.8cm (88mm) anti-aircraft gun pictured here. Despite this, the planners of Operation MARKET were confident that Allied air superiority could suppress such weapons during the airborne phase. *(Pierre-Olivier Buan)*

(**Opposite, above**) Operation MARKET was the largest airborne operation ever conducted over a multi-day period, with approximately 20,000 paratroopers taking part and almost another 15,000 personnel delivered to their objectives by gliders. In this picture, we see a squad of glider infantrymen in a CG-4A glider. Note the Browning Automatic Rifle (BAR), and the early-model 2.36in Rocket-Launcher M1A1. *(National Archives)*

(**Opposite, below**) American paratroopers are shown conferring with a group of young Dutch civilians over their map. To aid communication with the civilians in occupied Holland during Operation MARKET, Royal Dutch Commandos accompanied units in the 82nd and 101st airborne divisions, down to battalion level. Dutch-speaking personnel of the two American airborne divisions were also recruited to act as interpreters. *(National Archives)*

(**Above**) Another mortar in the airborne division inventory was the 60mm M2 pictured here. In both the October 1942 and February 1944 airborne division TO&Es there were seventy-five authorized. PIRs each had twenty-seven and GIRs twenty-four. The 60mm mortar M2 weighed only 42lb assembled and had a maximum range of 2,000 yards, firing a high-explosive (HE) round. (*National Archives*)

(**Opposite, above**) Glider infantrymen of the 101st are shown in this image, having landed in occupied Holland on 18 September 1944. Per the August 1944 airborne division TO&E, there were 345 Jeeps authorized. Each GIR had twenty-one and each PIR had fifteen. The majority of the Jeeps (111) were located in the divisional artillery where they were employed as prime movers (towing vehicles) or for hauling ammunition. (*National Archives*)

(**Opposite, below**) To increase the amount of cargo the airborne divisions' 0.25-ton trucks could transport, the October 1942 and February 1944 airborne division TO&Es authorized a total of 215 0.25-ton trailers, with two examples pictured here. The airborne division's anti-aircraft battalion had forty-four of them, with the divisional artillery having thirty-five authorized. (*National Archives*)

Taken on 19 September 1944, the third day of Operation MARKET GARDEN, is this photograph of Brigadier General James M. Gavin, commander of the 82nd, and the commander of the British Army 1st Airborne Corps, Lieutenant General Frederick Browning. For the duration of Operation MARKET GARDEN both the 82nd and 101st were overseen by Browning and not the US Army XVIII Airborne Corps. (*National Archives*)

(**Opposite, above**) To make up for the lack of any armoured fighting vehicles, at some point in time after Operation NEPTUNE, the reconnaissance platoon of the 82nd fielded a small number of machine-gun-armed Jeeps, with some crudely-affixed armour plates. In this picture we see a military vehicle collector has taken the time to recreate one of those wartime armoured Jeeps employed by the 82nd during its time in the ETO. (*Pierre-Olivier Buan*)

(**Opposite, below**) A serious threat to the paratroopers and glider infantrymen of the two American airborne divisions involved in Operation MARKET were German self-propelled anti-aircraft vehicles, armed with single or multiple-barrel 20mm automatic cannon. Pictured here is an example of the improvised nature of some of those vehicles, in this case manned by Waffen SS re-enactors during an historical military vehicle rally. (*National Archives*)

(**Opposite, above**) All the aircraft of the Troop Carrier Command assigned to Operation MARKET were committed to ferrying additional paratroopers and glider infantrymen to Holland over a period of several days, to the exclusion of all else. Therefore 248 B-24H Liberator bombers, as pictured here, were modified to drop parachute supply containers to the 82nd and 101st on 18 September 1944. German anti-aircraft defences shot down 7 and damaged another 160 of the bombers. (*USAF Museum*)

(**Opposite, below**) The bulk of the enemy forces confronting the 82nd and 101st in Operation MARKET were under the command of *Generaloberst* Kurt Student and consisted of the remnants of three German *Fallschirmjäger* (paratrooper) divisions, such as the men pictured here. To fill these out with sufficient manpower, personnel from paratroop training and replacement units based in Holland were also pressed into front-line service. (*National Archives*)

(**Above**) A typical tank employed by the Guards Armoured Division assigned to pass over one of the Dutch bridges captured by the 82nd and 101st during Operation GARDEN was the 'Firefly' pictured here. The Guards Armoured Division linked up with the 82nd on 19 September 1944, and through their combined efforts captured the two Dutch bridges at Nijmegen on the evening of 20 September 1944. (*Pierre-Olivier Buan*)

(**Above**) The initial joy expressed by the Dutch on the arrival of the Allied airborne and ground forces with Operation MARKET GARDEN had to be tempered by the widespread destruction inflicted upon their towns and cities during the fighting. An example of that devastation is visible in this picture of Nijmegen, with one of its two bridges in the background. (*National Archives*)

(**Opposite, above**) Some felt that the US Army airborne divisions required a tank of their own, which would be air-transportable. The eventual outcome was the development and production of the M22 Light Tank seen here, armed with a 37mm main gun. Obsolete even before production began in April 1943, it would never see combat with the US Army airborne divisions. (*Pierre-Olivier Buan*)

(**Opposite, below**) The plan for transporting the M22 Light Tank to the battlefield rested on the USAAF fielding the four-engine C-54 Skymaster pictured here. The interior fuselage of the aircraft proved too small for the complete tank. The army experimented with attaching the tank's hull to the underside of the C-54's fuselage and carrying the turret inside the aircraft. The tank was to be reassembled on landing at a captured enemy airfield. (*USAF Museum*)

The sector of the US Army's front lines that Hitler and his generals selected for the counter-offensive was in the heavily-forested region of the Ardennes, located in Belgium and Luxembourg. The Germans began their attack on 16 December 1944, and on 19 December 1944 surrounded and forced to surrender two of the three regiments of the inexperienced 106th Infantry Division. Pictured here are a few of the 6,000 American soldiers of the 106th marched into captivity that day. (*National Archives*)

(**Opposite, above**) The October 1942 and February 1944 airborne division TO&Es called for a total of eight liaison aircraft. A typical wartime example in the ETO was the L-4 Cub seen here, nicknamed the 'Grasshopper'. In both US Army armoured and infantry divisions of the Second World War, these were normally found in the divisional artillery element, serving as artillery spotting aircraft. (*National Archives*)

(**Opposite, below**) In late August 1944, Hitler and his senior staff considered whether it would be better to launch a large armour-led counter-offensive against the Red Army on the Eastern Front or against the Allied armies on the Western Front. After much thought, they concluded that a successful attack on the Western Allies might achieve a strategic decision. Leading that planned counter-offensive would be more than 1,000 tanks, such as the Panther pictured here, as well as assault guns and tank destroyers. (*Tank Museum*)

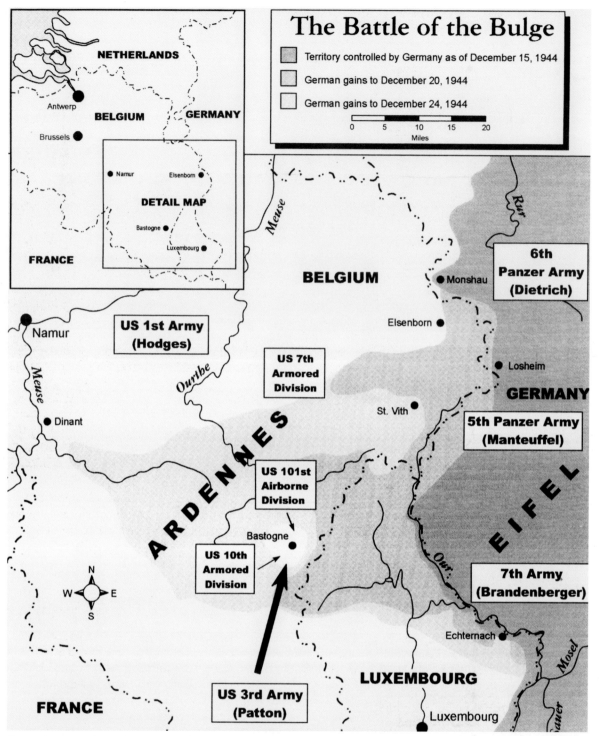

The Battle of the Bulge

- ▨ Territory controlled by Germany as of December 15, 1944
- ▤ German gains to December 20, 1944
- ☐ German gains to December 24, 1944

```
0    5    10    15    20
            Miles
```

NETHERLANDS

Antwerp

BELGIUM   GERMANY

Brussels

DETAIL MAP

Namur   Elsenborn

Bastogne

FRANCE   Luxembourg

BELGIUM

Monshau

Elsenborn

Losheim

6th Panzer Army (Dietrich)

GERMANY

Rur

Meuse

Namur

US 1st Army (Hodges)

US 7th Armored Division

St. Vith

5th Panzer Army (Manteuffel)

Ouribe

Meuse

Dinant

US 101st Airborne Division

A R D E N N E S

E I F E L

US 10th Armored Division

Bastogne

Our

7th Army (Brandenberger)

US 3rd Army (Patton)

Echternach

Mosel

LUXEMBOURG

FRANCE

Luxembourg

Shown here are the various stages of the German December 1944 counter-offensive and some of the key geographic locations of the series of battles known as the 'Battle of the Bulge'. To delay the German counter-offensive and provide time for the US Army to regroup and eventually counter-attack, the 82nd and 101st (in theatre reserve) were rushed forward to secure key road junctions in the Ardennes near St. Vith and at Bastogne. (*Author's collection*)

Both the 82nd and the 101st were rushed into the Ardennes aboard trucks and trailers from their bases near Rheims, France. Both units reached their respective areas of responsibility on 18 December 1944, and quickly set up defensive positions alongside other US Army units. (*National Archives*)

Because Major General Maxwell Taylor, divisional commander of the 101st, was in the United States when the German counter-offensive began, command of the division fell to Brigadier General Anthony C. McAuliffe, the 101st artillery commander, pictured here. As Lieutenant General Matthew B. Ridgway, commander of the XVIII Airborne Corps, was in England when the Germans struck, Major General James Gavin, in command of the 82nd, also became acting XVIII Corps commander. (*National Archives*)

Besides the 101st in Bastogne, there were a wide variety of other types of units in place, all of which would come under the command of Brigadier General Anthony C. McAuliffe. This included fifty-four units of the M18 Gun Motor Carriage (GMC) as seen here, best known by its unofficial nickname of the 'Hellcat'. The 76mm main gun-armed vehicles belonged to the 705th Tank Destroyer Battalion. (Bob Fleming)

Also falling under the command of the 101st while defending Bastogne were approximately fifty tanks of Combat Command B of the 10th Armored Division and Combat Command R of the 9th Armored Division. These would have included the M4 medium tank series, as pictured here, and M5 series light tanks. The former were armed with either a 75mm or 76mm main gun and the latter with a 37mm main gun. (Pierre-Olivier Buan)

The Germans surrounded Bastogne on 21 December 1944. The town's defenders, however, were able to maintain radio contact throughout the siege with their corps command and knew that a relief column from Lieutenant General George S. Patton's Third Army would soon be pushing towards them. Pictured here is a 75mm Pack Howitzer M1A1, which remained in the airborne division TO&E till the end of the war in the ETO. (*National Archives*)

The 105mm Howitzer M3 as pictured here was another of the 101st Airborne's artillery assets that helped to keep German ground forces from overrunning Bastogne. The weapon's barrel was the same as that of the standard 105mm towed howitzer, but shortened by 27in to reduce overall weight and allow it to fit within the confines of the CG-4A glider. (*National Archives*)

A key communication tool for every PIR and GIR company was the FM SCR-300 Radio, nicknamed the 'Walkie Talkie', seen here on the back of a US Army soldier. It weighed between 30lb and 40lb depending on the model, and had a maximum range of approximately 3 miles. It was typically fitted with a 33in whip antenna. Almost 50,000 were built between 1943 and 1945. (*National Archives*)

(**Opposite, above**) Another artillery asset within Bastogne under command of the 101st during the German siege was two armoured field artillery batteries, the 58th and the 420th, armed with the 105mm Howitzer Motor Carriage (HMC) M7 series. The open-topped vehicle, as pictured here, weighed approximately 51,000lb and had a crew of seven. The onboard howitzer had a maximum range of approximately 12,000 yards. (*Pierre-Olivier Buan*)

(**Opposite, below**) The largest artillery piece in Bastogne under the command of the 101st was the 155mm M1, an example of which is pictured here. These belonged to the 969th Field Artillery Battalion, which included remnants of two other 155mm M1-equipped field artillery battalions that were decimated by the initial German advance into the Ardennes. The 155mm M1 weighed in at approximately 9,500lb and fired a high-explosive (HE) round out to 16,000 yards. (*Pierre-Olivier Buan*)

Glider infantrymen of the 82nd march towards the defence of the small Belgian town of Werbomont, near the northern shoulder of the German penetration into US Army lines. Due to serious rear area logistical problems, the paratroopers and glider infantrymen of the 82nd and 101st, as well as all other US Army soldiers fighting in the Ardennes, lacked proper cold-weather gear until January 1945. (*National Archives*)

The Waffen SS armoured divisions in the northernmost portion of the German counter-offensive in the Ardennes included the *Jagdpanther* ('Hunting Panther') seen here. Disappointed in the poor anti-tank performance of the US Army's anti-tank rocket-launcher, Gavin had given permission for the men of the 82nd to use a large number of captured *Panzerfaust* ('tank fist' or 'armour fist') against their former owners. (*Liam Wilcox*)

Pictured is a sentry questioning the driver of a 0.25-ton truck. The sentry is armed with an M1 Garand rifle fitted with the Grenade Rifle, AT (Anti-tank), M9A1. It was not effective against late-war heavily-armoured German tanks and self-propelled guns, but could destroy lightly-armoured vehicles such as armoured cars and armoured half-tracks, or kill occupants of open-topped vehicles. (*National Archives*)

In this often-published image we see a paratrooper from the 82nd in the Ardennes. He is no doubt armed with an M1 Garand Rifle, but is also seen with the two-piece Rocket-Launcher 2.36in M9, which is evident from the fluted front portion of the weapon. The original one-piece, 2.36in Rocket-Launcher M1A1 lacked the fluted front end. A simple tube, the M9 only weighed 14.5lb. (*National Archives*)

Another wartime method for airborne division combat personnel to stop or delay armoured fighting vehicles, as it was for the rest of the US Army, was the anti-tank mine. In this picture an engineer is emplacing the Mine, Anti-tank, High-Explosive, M1A1 somewhere in the Ardennes. It weighed approximately 11lb and took 500lb of pressure to detonate. (*National Archives*)

(**Above**) To defend his position against three Waffen SS armoured divisions, Major General Gavin of the 82nd had taken under his command a number of non-airborne division assets, as had Brigadier General McAuliffe in Bastogne. These included a field artillery battalion armed with the 155mm Howitzer M1, as well as a tank destroyer battalion equipped with the M36 Gun Motor Carriage (GMC) seen here. (*Pierre-Olivier Buan*)

(**Opposite, above**) Encountered by the 82nd and 101st during the Battle of the Bulge were recently-formed *Volksgrenadier* divisions. These were about 10,000 men strong, compared to a standard German Army infantry division of approximately 17,000 men. To make up for the reduced personnel count, the *Volksgrenadier* divisions had a much larger complement of automatic weapons, such as the MG42 7.92mm machine gun seen here next to the deceased German soldier. (*National Archives*)

(**Opposite, below**) Due to a shortage of organic artillery support, the *Volksgrenadier* divisions that engaged in combat with the 82nd and 101st during the Battle of the Bulge had attached rocket *Werfer* (launcher) brigades. The most common rocket-projector employed by these units late-war was the towed 21cm *Nebelwerfer* ('smoke mortar'), a damaged example of which is pictured here. (*National Archives*)

The 101st and attached units in Bastogne ran desperately short of everything as the German encirclement of the town continued. On 22 December 1944 the 101st asked for an aerial supply mission to be put into action. With the weather clearing over the Ardennes, Troop Carrier Command pilots began dropping supplies over Bastogne the following day, as portrayed in this painting. (*US Army Center for Military History*)

(**Opposite, above**) To deliver the much-needed supplies to Bastogne, the pilots of the Troop Carrier Command had to run a gauntlet of German anti-aircraft guns. An example of what they encountered is the twin-mount 3.7cm *Flakzwiling* 43 pictured here. It had a theoretical rate of fire of 150 rounds per gun per minute. The guns were loaded from eight-round clips. (*National Archives*)

(**Opposite, below**) Pictured here is a C-47 Skytrain of the Troop Carrier Command that made a successful crash-landing near Bastogne after being struck by German anti-aircraft fire. Of the 927 re-supply missions flown to Bastogne between 23 and 27 December 1944, enemy anti-aircraft gunners accounted for 19 of the C-47 Skytrain aircraft. (*National Archives*)

Besides the aerial re-supply drops into Bastogne by the C-47 Skytrains of the Troop Carrier Command, sixty-one CG-4A gliders managed to land within the town's defensive perimeter between 23 and 27 December 1944. The enemy's anti-aircraft guns accounted for another seventeen shot down. The CG-4A glider pictured here brought in 155mm howitzer ammunition. (*National Archives*)

A litter party of medical corpsman (medics) is shown bringing a wounded man to a first-aid station in Bastogne. The airborne division headquarters, going back to the October 1942 TO&E, included a medical section, with each PIR and GIR authorized a 0.75-ton ambulance, which was not transportable by glider. The airborne division artillery battalion also had a medical section. (*National Archives*)

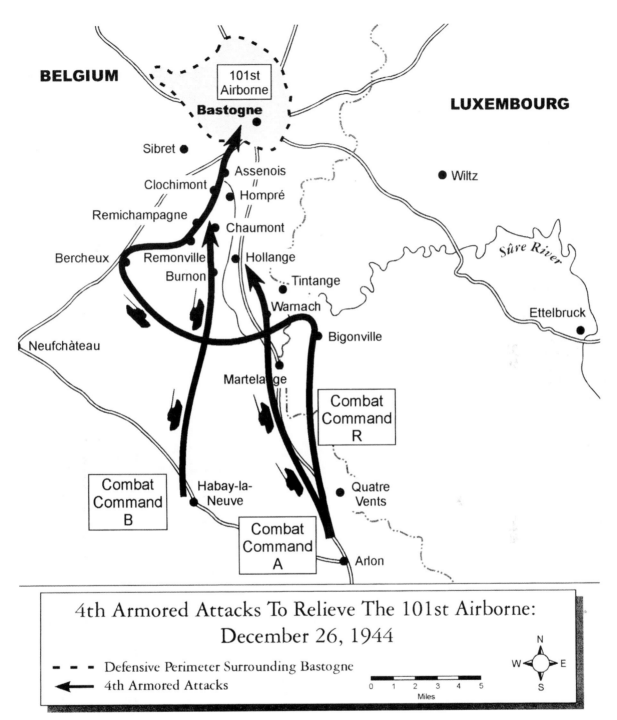

BELGIUM

LUXEMBOURG

101st Airborne

Bastogne

Sibret

Wiltz

Assenois

Clochimont

Hompré

Remichampagne

Chaumont

Bercheux

Remonville

Hollange

Burnon

Tintange

Sûre River

Warnach

Neufchâteau

Bigonville

Ettelbruck

Martelange

Combat Command R

Combat Command B

Habay-la-Neuve

Quatre Vents

Combat Command A

Arlon

4th Armored Attacks To Relieve The 101st Airborne: December 26, 1944

- - - Defensive Perimeter Surrounding Bastogne

◀— 4th Armored Attacks

N
W ◆ E
S

0 1 2 3 4 5
Miles

Patton's Third Army's relief of the 101st began on 22 December 1944 from an assembly area in Belgium, near the town of Arlo, located 20 miles south of Bastogne. Spearheaded by the 4th Armored Division, the assault was divided into three separate armoured columns, as shown on this map. The first of these three columns established contact with the 101st at 4.45 pm on 26 December 1944. (*National Archives*)

Pictured here is a preserved M4A3E2 that has had markings applied to replicate the first 4th Armored Division tank to break through to the 101st at Bastogne. The wartime example of the tank was commanded by First Lieutenant Charles Boggess, Jr. and was nicknamed 'Cobra King'. Lieutenant Boggess was welcomed to Bastogne by Lieutenant Webster of the 326th Engineers, 101st.

(Pierre-Olivier Buan)

With the October 1942 airborne division TO&E there were only two motorcycles authorized, both found in the Military Police platoon. With the large increase in personnel found in the December 1944 airborne division TO&E, the authorized motorcycle count went up to 260 units. Sixty-two were in the divisional artillery battalion and fifty-two in each PIR, but none were authorized for the GIR.

(Author's collection)

Patton's Third Army, which included the 17th Airborne Division, first became aware of the German forces in the Ardennes withdrawing on 11 January 1945. The next day, the Red Army launched a major offensive. On 14 January 1945, Hitler approved the withdrawal of the bulk of his forces from the Ardennes. On 16 December 1944, the siege of Bastogne was lifted. (*National Archives*)

(**Above**) Among the odd pieces of equipment in the airborne divisions' inventory was the man-portable flame-thrower, seen here during a training class. Three were authorized for the engineer battalion of the airborne divisions, beginning with the September 1942 TO&E. The airborne engineer battalion was also authorized four non-air-transportable 2.5-ton dump trucks. (*National Archives*)

(**Opposite, above**) Not taking any chances with Operation VARSITY, set for 24 March 1945, it was decided that all the airborne objectives would be in range of Allied artillery, such as the 8in Howitzer M1 pictured here. The weapon had a maximum effective range of approximately 18,000 yards. In addition to the artillery bombardment, almost 2,000 Allied fighters were assigned to suppress German ground defences. (*Pierre-Olivier Buan*)

(**Opposite, below**) Having just landed, the glider infantrymen of the 17th Airborne Division move out to do battle with the local German defenders during Operation VARSITY. To deliver the 17th Airborne Division to its chosen objectives, it was assigned 903 transport aircraft and 897 gliders. It was during Operation VARSITY that the C-46 twin-engine Commando first took part in an airborne operation. (*National Archives*)

Despite the heavy bombardment by Allied artillery and Allied fighter sweeps, conducted before the paratroopers and glider infantrymen of the 17th Airborne were delivered to their objectives, German anti-aircraft guns, such as the 20mm pictured here, took a heavy toll of both the low-flying transport planes and gliders, accounting for 54 shot down and approximately 400 damaged. (*National Archives*)

Almost 9,000 American paratroopers and approximately 5,000 glider infantrymen were transported to their objectives behind enemy lines on 23 March 1945 as part of Operation VARSITY. Total casualties for the 17th Airborne Division including killed, wounded or missing totalled around 1,500 men. By 27 March 1945, the German troops in the surrounding area began surrendering in large numbers as seen here. (*National Archives*)

In this photograph we see an American soldier embracing a Red Army soldier in celebration of the combined efforts of their armies, which brought an end to the Third Reich on 7 May 1945. The 82nd and 101st had total casualties, including killed, wounded and missing, of approximately 18,000 men. Reflecting its late-war commitment to combat, the 17th Airborne Division had about 13,000 total casualties by war's end in the ETO. (*National Archives*)

Chapter Three

The Cold War Era

With the end of the Second World War, the US Army dramatically shrank in size from a wartime high of 8 million men and 89 divisions to 591,000 men and ten divisions by early 1950. Of those ten active-duty divisions, seven were infantry divisions, one an armoured division and the remaining two airborne divisions, the 11th and the 82nd.

Despite the very mixed record of the airborne divisions during the Second World War, the army and the American public remained enamoured with them in the immediate post-war era. This was no doubt aided by the favourable publicity they had received for their exploits, and the fact that many of the wartime airborne officers had risen to prominent positions in the post-war army.

Reflecting the influence of the wartime airborne officers, one unrealistic plan never put into practice in the immediate post-war era called for every soldier in the army to be airborne-qualified. Another plan actually put into motion between 1946 and 1952 involved the conversion of four inactive part-time reserve infantry divisions into part-time reserve airborne divisions. The concept proved unworkable because there was insufficient time to qualify enough paratroopers during monthly drills.

Due to the limited budget available in early 1950, nine of the ten US Army divisions were under-strength. The 11th was a training division. Only the 82nd remained at full strength. The 82nd, based in the United States, along with three other non-airborne divisions, was considered a strategic reserve force in early 1950. On 21 May 1951, the XVIII Airborne Corps was reactivated to oversee the army's airborne divisions based in the United States.

Korean War

The US Army had five non-airborne divisions overseas performing occupation duties when the Korean War began on 25 June 1950. The 82nd would not participate in the Korean War due to its importance as the US Army's strategic reserve force. However, the 187th Airborne Infantry Regiment (AIR) of the 11th Airborne Division was detached and did serve in the conflict. It took part in only one airborne operation during the conflict, spending most of its time in the field as infantry.

With numerous attached units, the 187th Airborne Infantry Regiment was classified by the army as a Regimental Combat Team (RCT). The army employed RCTs during the Second World War up through to the Korean War. They were considered either temporary organizations for a specific mission or a semi-permanent organization that existed only in a specific theatre of operation for a certain duration of time.

New Post-War TO&E and Divisional Changes

Based on Second World War experiences, all three types of US Army divisions had their TO&Es changed in the immediate post-war period, with that of the airborne division being the most extensively changed. This appears in a US Army Center for Military History publication titled *Infantry, Part 1: Regular Army* by John K. Mahon and Romana Danysh:

> The first postwar airborne infantry TOEs did not appear until 1 April 1950, but airborne units had been organized earlier under draft tables similar to the final published tables … Both combat experience [Second World War] and tests conducted after the war at Fort Bragg, North Carolina, showed that they needed to be organized more like standard infantry units in order to be self-sustaining in ground operations over extended periods. The new TOEs, therefore, gave the airborne infantry more staying power and organized it along the same lines as the regular infantry, while retaining its special air assault capability.

The April 1950 airborne division TO&E meant that the 82nd possessed approximately the same manpower and equipment assets of the existing infantry divisions, which had a strength on paper of about 18,000 men.

In March 1951, the 11th was relieved of its training duties and once again brought up to full strength under the April 1950 airborne division TO&E. It was transferred to West Germany in 1956 where it replaced an infantry division. However, the higher cost of maintaining an airborne division and its unsuitability for many of the mission requirements in West Germany led to its deactivation on 1 July 1958.

Aircraft of the 1950s

The advent of larger US Air Force (USAF) transport planes at the end of the Second World War dispensed with the need for gliders. The first of these was the twin-engine, prop-driven 'C-82 Packet' that entered into production in June 1945. It had room for forty-one paratroopers or 20,000lb of air-droppable equipment and supplies.

Besieged by endless design flaws, an upgraded version of the C-82 Packet was the 'C-119 Flying Boxcar', which entered into production in 1947. It could transport forty-six paratroopers or 30,000lb of air-droppable equipment and supplies.

Introduced into service in 1950 was the four-engine, prop-driven 'C-124 Globe-master', which dwarfed all previous USAF transport aircraft. Not specifically designed for airborne division use, it was intended for strategic airlift purposes and could transport the trucks and tanks of the airborne divisions where needed, or 200 fully-equipped soldiers, to a paved runway.

Not specially designed for airborne division employment was the four-engine (both prop and jet) 'C-123 Provider', which initially entered into USAF service in 1955. Between the late 1970s and early 1980s some were pressed into service at Fort Bragg, North Carolina, the training centre of the airborne divisions, as aerial platforms from which paratroopers would make their initial training jumps.

Turbo-Prop-Engine-Powered Aircraft

In April 1956, the even larger four-engine 'C-133 Cargomaster' appeared. It was capable of transporting oversized equipment that the C-124 Globemaster could not. Both aircraft remained in service until the early 1970s. Unlike all the piston-engine-powered prop-driven USAF transport aircraft that came before it, the C-133 Cargomaster was powered by turbo-prop-driven engines. These offered increased range and more power for their weight than the older-generation piston-engine-powered counterparts.

In December 1956, the first model of the four-engine, turbo-prop-driven 'C-130 Hercules' series came off the production line. It could convey sixty-four paratroopers to their drop zone and up to 44,000lb of air-droppable equipment and supplies. Compared to the 1,770-mile range of the C-119 Flying Boxcar, the C-130 Hercules has a range of more than 2,500 miles on internal fuel tanks and almost unlimited range with in-flight refuelling.

Aircraft of the 1960s

A Canadian-designed aircraft adopted by the US Army in 1961 and capable of transporting up to twenty-six paratroopers was the 'C-7A Caribou'. It was a twin-engine, turbo-prop-driven utility transport plane capable of short take-off and landing (STOL) from unpaved runways. The US Army would transfer its inventory of 159 units of the C-7A Caribou to the USAF in 1967.

The year 1965 marked the introduction of the four-jet-engine 'C-141 Starlifter'. It was the replacement for the prop-driven C-124 Globemaster and C-133 Cargo-master. The C-141 was capable of delivering 123 paratroopers to their objective, as well as 71,000lb of air-transportable equipment and supplies by parachutes. As with the C-130 Hercules, the range of the C-141 Starlifter was almost unlimited with in-flight refuelling.

Appearing in 1969 was the first version of the massive 'C-5 Galaxy' series. Not intended to deliver paratroopers or be able to air-drop weapons and equipment by parachutes, the four-jet-engine-powered aircraft was intended to complement the C-141 in the strategic airlift role. Able to transport helicopters as well as tanks, the maximum take-off weight of the C-5 Galaxy is approximately 840,000lb.

Organizational Changes and New Weapons

The demise of the glider meant that there were no more GIRs in the airborne division TO&E; the PIRs found themselves relabelled Airborne Infantry Regiments (AIRs). The April 1950 airborne division TO&E called for three AIRs which, like their Second World War counterparts, were triangular in structure with each regiment further subdivided into three battalions and each battalion divided into three companies and so on down to squad level. Each battalion of the AIRs had the support of a heavy weapons company armed with machine guns, mortars and recoilless rifles.

The first recoilless rifles introduced into service with the airborne divisions were 57mm or 75mm in calibre and occurred at the very tail end of the Second World War. Post-war, both 90mm and 106mm recoilless rifles entered into service with the army's airborne divisions. The 90mm could be fired from the shoulder or the ground, whereas the size and weight of the 106mm recoilless rifle meant it that could only fire from a vehicle or a ground mount.

By the early 1970s, the 106mm recoilless rifle replacement in the airborne divisions proved to be the BGM-71 Tube-Launched, Optically Tracked, Wire-Guided (TOW) anti-tank missile. The TOW fired from either ground or vehicle mounts. It was also capable of being fired from helicopter gunships.

Equipment

While the infantry divisions' TO&E of 1950 called for a single organic medium tank battalion, the airborne divisions had two, although the tanks themselves were too large and heavy to be transported by the existing aerial assets. Rather, they were intended to join the airborne elements of the division upon securing their objectives. In 1954 the second medium tank battalion was dropped and replaced by regimental medium tank companies, which also remained non-air-transportable.

Included with the April 1950 airborne division TO&E were three artillery battalions armed with the towed 105mm howitzer and a single artillery battalion armed with the towed 155mm howitzer. Like the airborne division's medium tanks, the 155mm howitzer was too large and heavy to be air-transportable at that time.

There was also a towed 90mm anti-tank gun platoon added to the April 1950 airborne division TO&E; however, that particular weapon was a design failure and the anti-tank gun platoon had to make do with 105mm howitzers. A new addition to the April 1950 airborne division TO&E were two 4.2in mortar platoons to supplement the 81mm mortars in use since the Second World War.

Another TO&E Appears

As early as 1948, the US Army's senior leadership came to realize that tactical (battlefield) atomic bombs could play an important part in impending conflicts. This meant that the existing TO&Es of the US Army divisions might need adaption for future battlefields. Confirmation came from a series of exercises conducted between 1954 and 1955 under simulated atomic battlefield conditions. They convincingly demonstrated that the Second World War triangular divisional structure of the airborne and infantry divisions, modified for use by the US Army in the immediate post-war era, was obsolete, although that of the armoured divisions remained viable.

In September 1956, the 101st Airborne was reactivated to test the concept of a new TO&E for airborne divisions better suited for an atomic battlefield. It fell under a programme referred to as the Reorganization of the Airborne Division (ROTAD). It was very similar in concept to the Reorganization of the Current Infantry Division (ROCID) programme taking place at the same time but more austere in both men and equipment, with no organic tank battalions or regimental tank companies.

Under the ROTAD programme, the army's airborne divisions of approximately 11,000 men would only perform specialized airborne roles, followed by short periods of ground operations before being relieved. With this in mind, the support elements of the airborne division TO&E (artillery, anti-tank and logistical), reflecting the manpower and equipment shortages following the Korean War, were dramatically scaled back to the extent that they mirrored the October 1942 airborne division TO&E configuration favoured by McNair.

The Pentomic TO&E

On 20 December 1956, the US Army approved the new divisional TO&E for all its divisions, under the term 'Pentomic'. The army's three airborne divisions – the 11th, 82nd and 101st – were the first to be reconfigured to the Pentomic structure, with some of the army's other non-airborne divisions not reconfigured until 1958. Besides being able to function on the atomic battlefields, the Pentomic divisions were supposed to be able to perform equally well on conventional battlefields, ranging from low-intensity to mid-intensity conflicts.

In a US Army Center for Military History publication titled *The Evolution of US Army Tactical Doctrine 1946–1976* by Robert A. Doughty appears a description of the general structure of the new Pentomic airborne and infantry divisions:

> The new division consisted of five 'battle groups' which were relatively self-contained and semi-independent units including many of the support elements previously found in the regimental combat team. The basic component of the division was the infantry battle group which was larger than the previous battalion but smaller than a regiment. Each battle group contained five rifle

companies, a combat support company (including a mortar battery), and a headquarters and service company. The battle group was directly controlled by the division commander, though special task forces of two or more battle groups could be formed under an assistant division commander.

Nuclear Weapons for the Airborne Divisions

An important addition to the December 1956 Pentomic division TO&E was the army's first nuclear-capable surface-to-surface unguided rocket system, the MGR-1, mounted on a 6 × 6 truck and officially nicknamed the 'Honest John'. It was in production from 1953 until 1965 and was also capable of firing unguided rockets with a conventional or chemical warhead.

Following the Honest John into service was the 'M29 Davy Crockett Weapon System', which consisted of a recoilless rifle firing a small spigot nuclear warhead from a tripod or a 4 × 4 truck. It served with the army's airborne divisions from 1956 until 1968.

Another unguided rocket system, capable of being armed with a nuclear warhead, was the MGR-3, officially nicknamed the 'Little John'. It consisted of a small lightweight two-wheel trailer that had a launching rail for an unguided nuclear-warhead-armed rocket. It was in service with the army's airborne divisions from 1961 until 1969.

Let Us Try Again

Many within the senior ranks of the US Army had expressed doubts about the viability of the Pentomic division concept before its implementation. It proved an efficient arrangement for the airborne divisions, but far less so for the non-airborne divisions. They found it difficult to make it work in other than a possible atomic battlefield.

Despite some changes made to the Pentomic division TO&E, the army was already thinking of a new TO&E for its divisions. Therefore a new divisional TO&E was announced on 25 May 1961 and labelled the Reorganization Objective Army Division (ROAD). With the ROAD division, the US Army established four different types of divisions: airborne, infantry, mechanized infantry and armoured.

The basic feature of the new ROAD division was a common division base consisting of three brigades, to which a varying number of manoeuvre battalions (from two to five) – be they infantry, mechanized infantry or armour – could be attached, depending on mission requirements.

In a US Army Combat Studies Institute Report titled *Sixty Years of Reorganizing for Combat: A Historical Trend Analysis* appears this passage: 'The ROAD division was the lineal descendant of the 1943 armored division that the Army's senior leadership knew from the service in World War Two.'

ROAD Brigades

The three brigade headquarters elements of the ROAD divisions reported directly to the divisional commander and his staff. The artillery and other support elements of the ROAD divisions were considered part of their base structure, but could be parcelled out to the attached manoeuvre battalions in various unit configurations.

Brigades themselves were a command level element (above the regimental level and below that of the division) employed by the US Army infantry divisions of the First World War through to the beginning of the Second World War. They were done away with on the advent of the triangular infantry and airborne TO&Es first put in place in 1942, which had the three regimental headquarters elements report directly to the divisional commander and his staff.

The M56 Scorpion

In 1948, the US Army established a requirement for an air-transportable self-propelled 90mm anti-tank gun capable of parachute delivery at the onset of an airborne operation. It was intended to replace the airborne divisions' recoilless rifles in the anti-tank role.

On 16 February 1950, the Ordnance Branch of the US Army initiated the development of a vehicle labelled the Carriage, Motor, 90mm Gun, T101. The vehicle was later reclassified as the Gun, Self-Propelled, Full Tracked, 90mm, M56 on 2 November 1950 and received the official nickname 'Scorpion'.

A total of 160 units of the Scorpion came off the assembly lines between December 1957 and June 1958, enough for three airborne division battalions. Due to weight and size constraints, it had no armour protection. The weight restraint on the Scorpion design also meant that the recoil of its powerful forward-firing 90mm gun would raise the front of the lightweight vehicle off the ground when fired.

Scorpion Replacement

Even before the first production example of the Scorpion rolled off the assembly line, it was already considered obsolete by the US Army. This initiated the development of a new more modern vehicle referred to as an 'Airborne Assault Weapon System', beginning on 6 April 1956. This programme ended quickly due to a lack of funding.

Despite the cancellation of the Airborne Assault Weapon System, the Ordnance Department pushed ahead with the development of an armoured, full-tracked, air-transportable and air-droppable vehicle for airborne divisions, which would also equip the US Army's armoured cavalry regiments.

The M551 Sheridan

The initial authorization for a new armoured airborne tank was approved in 1956, which at the time was labelled the Airborne Assault Weapon System. It then became the 'Armored Reconnaissance/ Airborne Assault Vehicle' (AR/AAV) in January 1959. The pilot vehicles were designated the XM551.

The first two production examples of the AR/AAV were completed in July 1966, designated the M551 and officially nicknamed the 'Sheridan'. With the advent of the Sheridan, the Scorpion was eventually retired from service.

Armed with a 152mm combination gun and anti-tank guided missile-launcher, 1,662 units of the Sheridan came off the factory floor by 2 November 1970. When employed by airborne divisions it could be delivered to its objectives by parachute, referred to as the Low-Velocity Air Drop (LVAD) or Low-Altitude Parachute Extraction System (LAPES), both via the Lockheed C-130 Hercules.

Despite numerous upgrades and improvement over the decades, the Sheridan remained a troublesome and unreliable vehicle throughout its time in service. The majority of the fleet was retired from the inventory by 1979 and placed into storage. The last seventy units continued in service with the 82nd until 1997.

Other Options
As the Sheridans of the 82nd continued to age ungracefully, by the mid-1980s the army began considering other options. One was to take into service in 1986 a small number of 8 × 8 Marine Corps Light Armored Vehicles-25 (LAV-25) armed with a 25mm main gun. The LAV-25s tested by the 82nd received the designation M1047.

For a number of reasons – lack of fire-power, poor off-road mobility, too top-heavy in being LAPES – the army decided that the M1047 was not a suitable replacement for the Sheridan and ended the test. Strangely enough, in 2016 the 82nd began testing the M1047 once again, and in 2017 took a small number into service.

Back into Combat
The first post-Second World War divisional-sized combat action conducted by one of the army's airborne divisions took place in 1965. A civil war had erupted on 26 April 1956 in the Dominican Republic. To restore order and the leadership favoured by the American government, the 82nd was committed to what was referred to as Operation POWER PACK, along with Marine Corps units.

The initial US Army portion of Operation POWER PACK involved only a single airborne battalion of the 82nd, which landed by aircraft on 28 April and secured an airport east of the country's capital of Santo Domingo. By the following month, the remainder of the division arrived in the Dominican Republic.

With the loss of sixty members of the 82nd and an unknown number of anti-government rebels killed, order was eventually restored to the country by September 1965, with the installation of a new government acceptable to the American government. At this point Operation POWER PACK ended and the 82nd returned to the United States.

South-East Asia and the 101st

It was the Vietnam War that brought both of the army's two airborne divisions back into the line of fire. The first of the 101st's three airborne brigades arrived in South Vietnam in July 1965 and the last in late 1967. All were quickly pushed into action as light infantry forces as neither the terrain nor the nature of the fighting lent themselves to Second World War-type airborne operations.

An example of the fierce fighting that the men of the 101st dealt with in South Vietnam appears in this extract from the Medal of Honor citation of Lieutenant James A. Gardner for an action on 7 February 1966:

> During the attack, the enemy fire intensified. Leading the assault and disregarding his own safety, 1st Lt. Gardner charged through a withering hail of fire across an open rice paddy. On reaching the first bunker, he destroyed it with a grenade and without hesitation dashed to the second bunker and eliminated it by tossing a grenade inside. Then, crawling swiftly along the dike of a rice paddy, he reached the third bunker. Before he could arm a grenade, the enemy gunner leaped forth, firing at him. 1st Lt. Gardner instantly returned the fire and killed the enemy gunner at a distance of six feet. Following the seizure of the main enemy position, he reorganized the platoon to continue the attack. Advancing to the new assault position, the platoon was pinned down by an enemy machine gun emplaced in a fortified bunker. 1st Lt. Gardner immediately collected several grenades and charged the enemy position, firing his rifle as he advanced to neutralize the defenders. He dropped a grenade into the bunker and vaulted beyond. As the bunker blew up, he came under fire again. Rolling into a ditch to gain cover, he moved toward the new source of fire. Nearing the position, he leaped from the ditch and advanced with a grenade in one hand and firing his rifle with the other. He was gravely wounded just before he reached the bunker, but with a last valiant effort he staggered forward and destroyed the bunker and its defenders with a grenade. Although he fell dead on the rim of the bunker, his extraordinary actions so inspired the men of his platoon that they resumed the attack and completely routed the enemy. 1st Lt. Gardner's conspicuous gallantry was in the highest traditions of the U.S. Army.

By late 1967, the 101st was finding it impossible to train or acquire enough paratroopers to maintain the airborne status of its three airborne brigades. Combat losses, one-year tours of duty and competition from the 82nd and other army units for a shrinking pool of qualified paratroopers all contributed to this situation. This led to the US Army decision in January 1968 to convert the division into an 'airmobile division', which would depend on a fleet of helicopters to move around the battlefield.

The actual conversion of the 101st from an airborne division into an airmobile division began in July 1969. The division was then re-designated the 101st Airborne

Division (Airmobile), although it was designated in 1969 for a short time as the 101st Air Cavalry Division.

At the time that the 101st became an airmobile division, the most numerous helicopter in service was the UH-1 series, officially nicknamed the 'Iroquois' but better known by its unofficial nickname of the 'Huey'. It served in both the troop transport role and that of gunship. Eventually, the gunship role in the division was taken over by the 'AH-1 Cobra', beginning in 1968.

Airmobile Origins

The concept of a new type of army division based around the helicopter had begun in the early 1960s. In February 1963 the 11th, deactivated in 1956, was reactivated as an experimental division and referred to as the 11th Air Assault Division (Test). Employing both computers for war-gaming and ever-larger field exercises, the concept was judged a success by the army's leadership. As a result, the 11th Air Assault Division (Test) was deactivated in June 1965, with its men and equipment being absorbed into the newly-formed 1st Cavalry Division (Airmobile) in July 1965.

Other Airborne Formations in South-East Asia

Only a single brigade of the 82nd was ever committed to combat in South Vietnam. It was in response to the enemy's surprise countrywide 'Tet Offensive' that had begun on 30 January 1968 and unfolded in three phases, which lasted until 23 September 1968. The first elements of the single 82nd Division airborne brigade transferred to South Vietnam arrived in the country on 14 February 1968.

To make up for the loss of the single airborne brigade of the 82nd sent overseas and to keep the division in the United States at full strength, a fourth airborne brigade was activated to replace it. That fourth airborne brigade was inactivated upon the return of the single airborne brigade from South Vietnam in December 1969.

In addition to the various brigades of the 82nd and 101st that saw action during the Vietnam War, there existed a third independent airborne brigade designated the 173rd (Separate), which also served during the conflict. It was similar in concept to the 187th Regimental Combat Team, which served during the Korean War and was intended in theory for operations that did not warrant the commitment of an airborne division.

More TO&E Changes

When the last elements of the 101st Airborne Division (Airmobile) returned from South Vietnam to the United States in 1972, it consisted of three brigades, two airmobile and one airborne. It was at this point that it was reorganized to bring it up to the ROAD standards. This appears in an extract from a US Army Center for

Military History publication titled *Maneuver and Firepower: The Evolution of Divisions and Separate Brigades* by John B. Wilson:

> The airborne division was the last type of division to be modernized. As in other divisions, the new tables provided an air defense artillery battalion, adjutant general, and finance company, and a materiel management company ... The most significant change, however, was the replacement of the supply company with a supply and service battalion, which provided the division with over 500 additional service personnel.

In 1974, the 101st was re-designated the 101st Airborne Division (Air Assault), and the single remaining airborne brigade had its jump status removed and was converted into an airmobile brigade, the retention of the word 'airborne' in its 101st designation now being only an honorary historical reference. From a US Army manual titled *Air Assault Operation* dated 2011 appears this passage:

> An air assault is a vertical [helicopter] envelopment conducted to gain a positional advantage, to envelop or to turn enemy forces that may or may not be in a position to oppose the operation. Ideally, the commander seeks to surprise the enemy and achieve an unopposed landing when conducting a vertical envelopment. However, the assault force must prepare for the presence of opposition. At the tactical level, vertical envelopments focus on seizing terrain, destroying specific enemy forces, and interdicting enemy withdrawal routes.

The 82nd, with nine airborne infantry battalions and an armour battalion, also adopted the same new ROAD TO&E, as did the 101st, in 1974. The major difference was that the 101st had two aviation brigades and the 82nd only a single aviation battalion.

Quick Reaction Force (QRF)

In 1958, the XVIII Airborne Corps was assigned an additional mission as the Strategic Army Corps (STRAC). Its role, according to a RAND Corporation report, was to 'deter or suppress small wars before they turned into large wars.' It originally consisted of the 82nd and 101st as well as two non-airborne divisions. The RAND Corporation, founded in 1949, is a civilian think-tank funded by the American government as well as private endowments and often employed by the US Army to research policy and doctrine.

As the US Army had not acquired the approval of the Joint Chiefs of Staff (JCS) for the forming of STRAC, neither the USAF nor the US Navy was obliged to provide any transportation assets unless the American Congress approved an official state of war. With the forming of the joint US Strike Command (STRICOM) in 1961, this oversight stood corrected.

Due to a number of unexpected events in the Middle East in the late 1970s, the American government called for a replacement for the US Strike Command (STRICOM). As originally conceived in 1978, it consisted of the 82nd, the 101st and a single US Marine Corps (USMC) division and its assigned name was the 'Rapid Deployment Force'.

The Rapid Deployment Force concept was not well-received by many in the senior levels of the American military as it lacked the transportation assets for the roles conceived for it. In 1980, with some refinements, it became the 'Rapid Deployment Joint Task Force' (RDJTF), which now included all the services as indicated by the term 'joint' in its name.

The original intention was that no specific military force be a permanent part of the RDJFT. However, the reality was that only the 82nd and the 101st fit into the roles assigned to the RDJFT. In 1983 it received the new title of the 'United States Central Command' (USCENTCOM), which is currently an 'area of responsibility' (AOR) upper-level command-level element of the American military, one of fifteen.

The Army of Excellence

With the end of the Vietnam War, the US Army turned its attention once again to the threat posed to Europe by the Soviet Army. In the aftermath of the 1973 Yom Kippur War, the US Army took it upon itself to evaluate ROAD and found it wanting in certain respects. To correct these perceived shortcomings, the US Army, more so among the heavy divisions rather than airborne, came up with a new concept titled 'Division 86' in 1974. It was so-named because 1986 was as far in the future as the army's leadership could project the Soviet threat.

In 1982–83, the first of the army's heavy divisions began the transition from the ROAD TO&E to the Division 86 TO&E. In the end, however, the Division 86 concept proved unworkable at the heavy divisional level and was never fully implemented. Rather, a new divisional concept referred to as the 'Army of Excellence' (AOE) appeared in 1983.

From a US Army historical monograph titled *The Army of Excellence: The Development of the 1980s Army* by John L. Romjue there appears the following passage describing the changes to the 82nd with the new AOE division concept:

Airborne division changes included provision for effective on route communications for divisional units, tailoring of the nuclear-biological-chemical company, an increase in anti-armor strength, additional helicopter lift capacity and an additional medical company, and a pathfinder platoon. Nonorganic organizations considered by the AOE planners to require a high degree of habitual association with the airborne division were a rigger company, mobile protected gun battalions, and a truck company. Parachute qualification remained the division's outstanding special training requirement. As configured at this point, the light infantry division (airborne) would be a nine-battalion organization 10,856 strong.

Rotor-Wing Units

The actual restructuring of the 82nd and the 101st to the AOE TO&E did not begin until 1985. In 1986, a major change to all the army's various types of divisions (except the 101st) under the AOE TO&E proved to be the addition of an aviation brigade. Rather than the three-brigade structure in place since the Pentomic TO&E, the division now had four brigades with the advent of the AOE TO&E. The 101st retained its two aviation brigades, making it a five-brigade division under the AOE TO&E.

Labelled by one army general as 'a manoeuvre element capable of multifunctional uses', the aviation brigades differed between that of the 82nd and the 101st. Those of the 82nd consisted of a headquarters and headquarters company (HHC), a reconnaissance squadron, one attack helicopter battalion and two assault helicopter companies, totaling 978 personnel. Those of the 101st Division's turned out to be larger and therefore consisted of more helicopters and personnel.

The aviation brigades flew a number of different types of helicopters. For the reconnaissance squadron, there was the 'OH-58D Kiowa' that had first entered into army service in 1984. The attack helicopter battalion flew the 'AH-64A Apache', which had entered into production in 1983. The assault helicopter companies operated the 'UH-60A Black Hawk' and the 'CH-46 Chinook', which first entered into production in 1962.

The 82nd in the Caribbean

Continued political disorder on the small Caribbean island of Grenada in 1983 attracted the attention of the American government. Concerned about a growing Cuban/Soviet influence in the region, a decision came about for military intervention. This resulted in Operation URGENT FURY, which was a large-scale joint service operation that lasted from 25 October 1983 until 15 December 1983.

The 82nd eventually contributed four airborne battalions to Operation URGENT FURY. At first the plans called for the leading elements of the division to parachute in to capture the island's major airport. However, at the last minute, it was assigned to two US Army Ranger battalions.

Grenada was secured by the 82nd in early November 1983, with the last battalion returning to the United States on 12 December 1983. Losses for the division were 19 killed and 116 wounded, with 16 of those killed in a friendly-fire incident. Causalities among the hostile Grenadian forces, a small contingent of 64 Cuban Army soldiers and almost 1,000 armed Cuban construction workers on the island that resisted the American forces, came out at approximately 500 personnel.

The 82nd in Central America

On the night of 20 December 1989, a brigade of the 82nd parachuted onto Torrijos International Airport, Panama as part of a large-scale, joint-service endeavour code-named Operation JUST CAUSE. Its goal was to remove the military leader of the country who had become unfriendly to American government interests and restore local leadership more attuned to those interests.

After the nighttime combat jump into Panama, the first since the Second World War, and the seizure of the country's international airport, the 82nd conducted a series of follow-on helicopter assault missions in Panama City, the nation's capital, and in the surrounding areas, dismantling the bulk of the nation's military forces within the first twenty-four hours.

Operation JUST CAUSE ended on 3 January 1990, with the 82nd units that had taken part returning to the United States in early January 1990. Some 200 to 300 Panamanian combatants died for the loss of twenty-three American military personnel, with three belonging to the 82nd.

Sheridans in Panama

An important milestone for the 82nd during Operation JUST CAUSE was the fact that it successfully air-dropped eight out of ten Sheridans into Panama on 20 December 1989. The parachutes on one of the ten vehicles failed to deploy and it was destroyed on impact, while another was badly damaged on landing and rendered inoperable.

During the fighting that followed, the Sheridans of the 82nd employed their 152mm conventional rounds against the stout headquarters building of the Panamanian defence forces, referred to as *La Commandancia*, with great effect. This appears in a passage from the March-April 1990 issue of *ARMOR* magazine in an article 'Sheridans in Panama' by Captain Kevin J. Hammond and Captain Frank Sherman:

> The Sheridans engaged *La Commandancia* at 1445 and fired ten rounds of 152mm HEAT with devastating results. The HEAT rounds penetrated the 10-inch reinforced concrete walls and caused extensive damage to the interior structure of the building. The commander's intent, to expend a few well-placed main gun rounds rather than to risk the lives of infantrymen to clear the buildings, was accomplished.

In an after-action report on Operation JUST CAUSE appears this passage: 'Once Sheridans moved into an area or after an initial engagement involving the M551A1s, enemy forces generally refused to fire or snipe at convoys or positions in the vicinity of the Sheridans.'

Airborne Divisions in the Middle East

Following Saddam Hussein of Iraq's ill-conceived plan to invade the neighbouring country of Kuwait on 2 August 1990, the American government feared that his next move would be to invade Saudi Arabia and they therefore dispatched the first elements of the 82nd. They arrived in Saudi Arabia starting on 8 August 1990, followed by the remainder of the division. It and the later arriving 101st, along with some other non-airborne units, would be under the oversight of the XVIII Airborne Corps.

The reality was that the 82nd was not up to realistically dealing with the armour and mechanized infantry divisions of the Iraqi Army, having only a single battalion of Sheridans. Its presence in Saudi Arabia was only intended as a 'trip-wire' to deter Saddam Hussein from invading the country until such time as the heavy (armoured and mechanized infantry) divisions of the US Army could arrive. This period received the code-name Operation DESERT SHIELD.

On 16 January 1991, the American military and those of its allied forces in the Middle East launched a massive, multi-service assault on Iraq, code-named Operation DESERT STORM. Leading the ground-assault phase were the men and helicopters of the 101st as seen in this passage from a US Army Center for Military History publication titled *War in the Persian Gulf: Operation Desert Shield and Desert Storm August 1990–March 1991*:

> The XVIII Airborne Corps' main attack, led by Major General J.H. Binford Peay III's 101st Airborne Division, was scheduled for 0500; but fog over the objective forced a delay. While the weather posed problems for aviation and ground units, it did not abate direct support fire missions. Corps artillery and rocket-launchers poured fire on the objective and approach routes. At 0705, Peay received the word to attack. Screened by Apache and Cobra attack helicopters, 60 Black Hawk and 40 Chinook choppers of the XVIII Airborne Corps' 18th Aviation Brigade began lifting the 1st Brigade into Iraq. The initial objective was Forward Operating Base (FOB) Cobra, a point some 110 miles into Iraq. A total of 300 helicopters ferried the 101st troops and equipment into the objective area in one of the largest helicopter-borne operations in military history.

In 100 hours (approximately four days) Iraq lost a good part of its military might and quickly asked for a ceasefire, which was approved. Of its 4,280 pre-DESERT STORM tanks it lost 3,877 during the fighting, half their fleet of approximately 3,000 armoured personnel carriers and almost all their 3,100 artillery pieces. Iraqi military casualties were estimated to be about 20,000 killed and another 75,000 wounded. The American military lost 148 military personnel during DESERT STORM, with 16 of those belonging to the 101st.

Reflecting its unsuitability for the highly-mobile ground campaign that characterized DESERT STORM, the 82nd played only a minor secondary role. It was attached to a French Army light armoured division in case it encountered any Iraqi Army armoured units. Lacking the ground transportation assets possessed by the heavy divisions of the US Army, it was assigned a number of US Army National Guard truck companies to help it keep up with the French Army division advance. The 82nd returned to the United States between 18 March and 22 April 1991 with no lives lost.

During the Korean War the C-46 Commando pictured here was preferred over the C-47 Skytrain for airborne operations. This could be attributed to its ability to carry more paratroopers than the C-47, and because it had two fuselage doors compared to the single fuselage door on the C-47. This meant that paratroopers on board the C-46 could exit the aircraft more quickly and land in tighter formations. (*USAF Museum*)

(**Opposite, above**) The only US Army airborne unit that took part in the Korean War was the 187th Airborne Infantry Regiment of the 11th. With various attached units, it became the 187th Regimental Combat Team (RCT). It arrived in South Korea in September 1950, but only took part in one major airborne operation in March 1951 that was code-named Operation HAWK. Pictured here are paratroopers of the 187th RCT during the Korean War. (*National Archives*)

(**Opposite, below**) The intended wartime replacement for the C-47 Skytrain and the C-46 Commando was the C-82 Packet pictured here. The prototype's initial flight was in September 1944, with the first production units being delivered in late 1945, too late to see use in combat. In the airborne operation role, it could deliver forty-one paratroopers, air-drop cargo through its two rear clam-shell doors and tow gliders. (*USAF Museum*)

(**Above**) In 1947, a much-improved model of the C-82 Packet, labelled the C-119 Flying Boxcar seen here, appeared in service with the United States Air Force (USAF), the successor to the United States Army Air Forces (USAAF). It was the C-119 that saw service in the airborne operation role during the Korean War and not the C-82. The introduction of the C-82 and C-119 made gliders no longer necessary. (*USAF Museum*)

Like its predecessor the C-82 Packet, the C-119 Flying Boxcar had two large clam-shell doors at the rear of its fuselage through which air-transportable cargo could be unloaded. Paratroopers exited the aircraft through two large doors at the rear of the fuselage and not the clam-shell doors. When transporting non-paratroopers, it had room for sixty-seven passengers or thirty-five stretcher cases.
(*USAF Museum*)

In this 1950s' era recruitment poster we see the US Army appealing to young men to join an elite organization with its own distinctive pieces of apparel. The uniform pictured was the standard enlisted man's wool serge uniform of the Second World War. The blue dickie and the blue piping on the overseas cap are the branch colours of the infantry. The shoulder patch represents the 82nd All-American Division.
(*82nd Division Museum*)

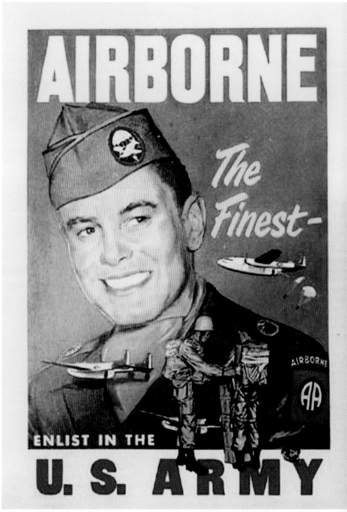

AIRBORNE
The Finest –
ENLIST IN THE
U.S. ARMY

The C-123 Provider shown here evolved from earlier designs for a large glider. The first prototype of a twin-engine prop-driven version flew in October 1949. To improve its performance, approximately 180 units were upgraded by the addition of two jet engines, one on either wing. Some eventually saw service in the training role, taking up new recruits to make their first jumps from an aircraft. *(USAF Museum)*

During the Second World War all the airborne division's heavier equipment, such as 6 × 6 trucks, had to be delivered from the United States via ship. With the advent of ever-larger prop-driven aircraft such as the C-124 Globemaster pictured here, which first entered into USAF service in 1950, there was now the option of delivering oversized cargo such as 6 × 6 trucks and even tanks to support overseas airborne operations. *(USAF Museum)*

In this no doubt staged photograph taken on the ground, we see a paratrooper wearing the post-war herringbone twill fatigues, which replaced the Second World War wool field uniforms, except in cold weather environments. He is outfitted with the post-war-introduced T-10 parachute. The black leather boots worn by the paratrooper in the picture mark it as being taken after 1957, when the army did away with the brown leather paratrooper boots.
(*National Archives*)

(**Opposite, above**) In this picture we see both paratroopers from the 82nd wearing what was labelled the Desert Battle Dress Uniform (DBDU). It was introduced into use in 1991 and unofficially nicknamed the 'chocolate chip camouflage'. The maroon beret visible in the picture was unofficially introduced for wear by airborne soldiers in the mid-1970s. It became an official uniform item in 1980. (*DOD*)

(**Opposite, below**) The soldier with his back to the camera, and the headphone set, is the aircraft's jumpmaster. He is typically an officer, or a senior non-commissioned officer (NCO), considered an expert in parachuting and responsible for the inspection of all the paratroopers' gear and equipment before boarding the aircraft. In the air he oversees their exit from the plane and deals with any last-minute problems. (*National Archives*)

(**Opposite, above**) The paratroopers in this picture have attached their static-line snap hooks to the aircraft's anchor-line cable just prior to exiting the plane at the jumpmaster's command. The paratroopers pictured are wearing a helmet made of Kevlar, first introduced into service in 1983. It and a protective vest were collectively referred to as the Personnel Armor System for Ground Troops (PASGT). (*DOD*)

(**Opposite, below**) The PASGT helmets seen here with these paratroopers prior to a jump were nicknamed 'the Fritz' by the American Press due to its resemblance to the German helmets of the Second World War. It was nicknamed the 'Kevlar' or the 'K-pot' by the soldiers. Those issued to paratroopers had a different internal suspension system from the version worn by non-airborne soldiers. (*DOD*)

(**Above**) The replacement for the C-47 Skytrain, C-46 Commando and the C-119 Flying Boxcar proved to be the C-130 Hercules transports pictured here. Unlike its predecessors, which were powered by two piston engines, the C-130 series was powered by four turboprop (gas turbine) engines, which provided a dramatic increase in performance. The prototype flew in 1954, with production beginning in 1956. In the airborne role, it could transport sixty-four paratroopers. (*DOD*)

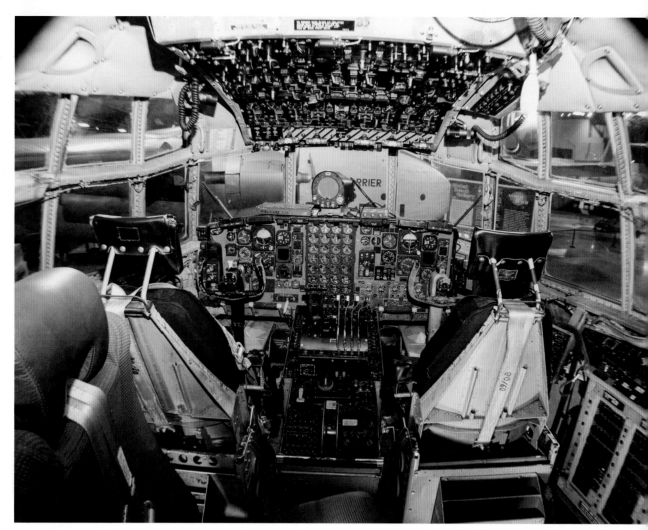

(**Above**) Visible is the analogue cockpit of an early-production example of the C-130 Hercules. Unlike the C-46 Commando and the C-47 Skytrain based on passenger plane designs, the C-130 was designed from the ground up as a military aircraft, capable of operating from unpaved runways. This was a design feature lacking in the C-46 and C-47, as well as the C-119 Flying Boxcar. (*USAF Museum*)

(**Opposite, above**) The C-130 can deliver various types of oversized equipment, such as the High Mobility Multipurpose Wheeled Vehicles (HMMWV), popularly known by their nickname of the 'Humvee'. In this photograph we see riggers during a training session on how to prepare an HMMWV for delivery by air. In the army, riggers are responsible for maintaining both parachutes and all other equipment employed in air-drops. (*DOD*)

(**Opposite, below**) The crew of a US Air Force transport plane is checking that the wheeled vehicles in the process of coming onboard their aircraft are securely attached to their drop pallets. When over the assigned delivery area either a small drogue chute or a steel cable will pull the pallets with cargo out the rear of the transport aircraft. Once clear of the plane a large twin parachute stored on the hood of the vehicles deploys. (*DOD*)

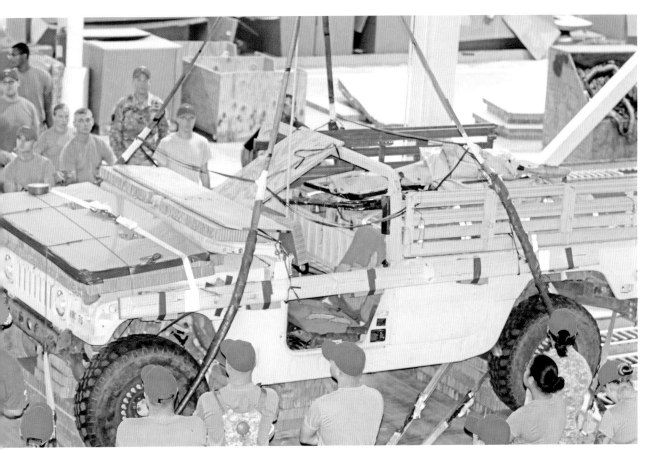

(**Above**) One method of delivering cargo or equipment from the C-130 Hercules is referred to as High Altitude Low Opening (HALO). It involves releasing a piece of equipment (secured to a pallet) as pictured, out of the rear open ramp of the aircraft. To facilitate its exit a small drogue parachute attached to the pallet is released. To ease the pallet's departure from the aircraft there are rollers on the fuselage floor of the C-130. (*DOD*)

(**Opposite, above**) Another method by which oversized cargo or equipment can be air-dropped by a C-130 Hercules is known as the Low Altitude Parachute Extraction System (LAPES), which is pictured here. It involves a C-130 Hercules flying extremely low and slow above a landing zone, at which point a drogue parachute is released through the open rear ramp of the aircraft, which in turn drags out a pallet with attached cargo or equipment upon rollers mounted in the fuselage floor. (*National Archives*)

(**Opposite, below**) The C-7A Caribou pictured here was designed and built by a Canadian firm. Its short take-off and landing (STOL) capabilities attracted the attention of the US Army, which acquired the first of 22 units in 1961, out of a total order of 159 examples. It was capable of carrying thirty-two passengers or twenty-six paratroopers, and could also deliver almost 9,000lb of cargo. (*USAF Museum*)

(**Opposite, above**) Looking for improved operational capabilities over the prop-driven C-124 Globemaster and the C-133 Cargomaster and the ability to deliver paratroopers around the globe, the USAF identified a requirement for a large jet-engine-powered transport in 1960, with the first flight of the prototype in 1963. The first of 285 units of the C-141 pictured here entered the USAF inventory in 1965. (*DOD*)

(**Above**) In this painting by Al Sprague titled 'Jump into Night', we see paratroopers from the 82nd exiting a C-141 Starlifter during the opening act of Operation JUST CAUSE, the American military invasion of Panama in December 1989. As with the nighttime air-drops conducted during the Second World War, a combination of poor weather conditions and navigation issues led to few of the 2,200 paratroopers of the 82nd landing where they should have done. (*US Army Center for Military History*)

(**Opposite, above**) The massive C-5 Galaxy pictured here was one of 181 units constructed for the USAF between 1968 and 1989. It was the jet-powered counterpart of the earlier C-133 Cargomaster in that it was large enough to carry all the existing US Army equipment, which the C-141 could not. However, pushing the design envelope with the C-5 led to large cost overruns and an endless series of technical problems. (*DOD*)

AIR FORCE RESERVE COMMAND

(**Above**) Unlike its smaller counterpart, the C-141 Starlifter, the C-5 Galaxy came with both a rear ramp and a front ramp that requires the entire nose of the plane to be raised as seen in this picture. Above the cargo deck that runs the length of the aircraft fuselage is another deck for up to seventy-five passengers. Despite numerous upgrades during its time in service, it continues to have serious maintenance and reliability issues. (*DOD*)

(**Opposite, above**) As with the Korean War, through to the early 1960s a great deal of the equipment and weapons in use by the army's airborne divisions dated from the Second World War. This can be seen in this picture of paratroopers in Lebanon in 1958. The soldier in the foreground is armed with the Browning Automatic Rifle (BAR), while the soldier in the background is armed with an M1 Garand Rifle. (*National Archives*)

(**Opposite, below**) The Pistol, Automatic (a misnomer) Caliber Model M1911A1, better known as the .45 or the .45 automatic, was an item that every US Army paratrooper in the Second World War had to have. It was officially replaced in the 1980s by the Pistol, Semi-automatic, 9mm, M9 seen here. Unlike the M1911A1 that had only a seven-round magazine, the M9 has a fifteen-round magazine. (*DOD*)

The Second World War-era M1 Garand Rifle would be replaced by the US Army in 1961 with the M14 Rifle seen here. The M14 Rifle was nothing more than an updated and modified version of the M1 Garand that was fed by a detachable twenty-round box that inserted into the underside of the weapon's receiver. Production of the M14 rifle continued until 1963. (DOD)

Because the M14 rifle proved inadequate during the early stages of the Vietnam War compared to the enemy's AK-47 assault rifles, a replacement labelled the M16 rifle was developed and first issued in 1964. It had a number of shortcomings that caused many American soldiers to doubt its reliability. This resulted in its replacement in 1969 by the M16A1 rifle seen here with US Army soldiers in South Vietnam. (National Archives)

The post-war replacement for both the air-cooled .30 calibre M1919A4 light machine gun and the water-cooled M1917A1 heavy machine gun in the army's airborne divisions was the M60 machine gun pictured here, which fired a 7.62mm round. It was introduced into service at the same time as the M14 rifle. Due to its weight and size it was nicknamed the 'Pig' by the soldiers during the Vietnam War. *(DOD)*

The 1984 replacement for the M60 machine gun in the airborne divisions was the M249 Squad Automatic Weapon (SAW) seen here, which fired a 5.56mm round. Work on the development of the M249 SAW began in 1966. The army was looking to boost the fire-power in its rifle squads with a light machine gun that had the ability to deliver sustained fire with ammunition fed to the receiver via a 200-round capacity magazine. *(DOD)*

In 1978, the US Army replaced the Second World War-era 60mm Mortar M2 with the much more capable 60mm M224 Mortar, seen here being carried by a soldier. The weapon weighs approximately 50lb when in firing order and is operated by a three-man crew. There is a full range of ammunition for the M242, including high-explosive, infrared and visible light illumination, and smoke. *(DOD)*

(**Opposite, above**) In use with airborne divisions from the Second World War until today is the Caliber .50 Browning Machine Gun Heavy Barrel (HB) M2 seen here on a private collector's M151 0.25-ton Utility Truck. Nicknamed the 'Ma Duce' or 'Cal Fifty', the weapon has a maximum effective range of 2,000 yards. The M151 entered US Army service in 1960 and served until the late 1980s in progressively improved models. *(Ian Wilcox)*

(**Opposite, below**) Not an organic weapon for the Second World War airborne divisions was the 4.2in (107mm) Mortar M2 fielded by the US Army in 1943. Nevertheless, its demonstrated effectiveness in combat led to the post-war adoption by the airborne divisions of its improved successor seen here, designated the 4.2in (107mm) Mortar M30, which appeared in service in 1951 in time for the Korean War. *(National Archives)*

The replacement for the Second World War-era 81mm Mortar M1 appeared in the 1960s and received the designation M29. However, by the 1970s the army began looking for another 81mm mortar that could fire a newly-developed generation of more powerful and longer-ranged rounds. The army eventually decided in 1987 on a licence-built copy of a British-designed 81mm mortar seen here. In American military service it is labelled the M252. (*DOD*)

(**Opposite, above**) Going back to the tail end of the Second World War, the US Army embraced the employment of recoilless rifles. At the time, it was the 57mm Recoilless Rifle M18 and the 75mm Recoilless Rifle M20. Those were eventually replaced in the post-war era by the 90mm Recoilless Rifle M67 pictured here, and the 106mm Recoilless Rifle M40. Due to its weight, the M40 could only be fired from a tripod or a vehicle mount. (*National Archives*)

(**Opposite, below**) In this picture we see an M151 0.25-ton Utility Truck belonging to the 82nd during Operation POWER PACK, the American military invasion of the Dominican Republic in May 1965. The vehicle is armed with the 106mm Recoilless Rifle M40. When the M40 was fired, the back-blast extended in a cone-shaped pattern up to 75 yards deep and 150 yards wide behind the weapon and alerted the enemy to its location. (*National Archives*)

(**Above**) The 1970 replacement for the 106mm Recoilless Rifle in the anti-tank role for the army was the BGM-71 Tube-Launched, Optically-Tracked, Wire-Guided (TOW) seen here mounted on an 82nd M151 0.25-ton Utility Truck. Due to its size and weight it had to be fired from a ground tripod or vehicle mount. It was also capable of being fired from helicopters. (*DOD*)

(**Opposite, above**) The 1963 replacement for the army's immediate post-war-era 3.5in M20 Rocket-Launcher was the one-shot, disposable M72 Light Anti-tank Weapon (LAW). Unhappiness with the weapon's poor armour penetration abilities led to the introduction in 1975 of the M47 Surface-Attack Guided Missile System, referred to as the 'Dragon'. It lasted in service with the army until 2001. (*DOD*)

(**Opposite, below**) The first short-range shoulder-fired surface-to-air anti-aircraft missile, placed into service by the army in 1968, was designated the FIM-43 Redeye. Beginning in 1981, it was replaced by a much-improved version originally labelled the 'Redeye II' but subsequently referred to as the FIM-92 Stinger seen here. Both anti-aircraft missiles employ infrared homing to acquire their targets. (*DOD*)

(**Opposite, above**) Not organic to Cold War-era airborne divisions was the MIM-72 medium-range Chaparral anti-aircraft missile system seen here. It would, however, be found at the XVIII Airborne Corps level. The vehicle chassis was based upon an unarmoured version of the M113 designated the M548. The surface-to-air missiles that armed the vehicle were a modified version of the AIM-9 air-to-air Sidewinder infrared homing missile. (*DOD*)

(**Opposite, below**) Another Cold War anti-aircraft weapon found at the XVIII Airborne Corps level was the MIM-23 Homing All-The-Way Killer (Hawk) pictured here, which entered service in 1959. It had a semi-active radar homing guidance system, with a range of approximately 15 miles in its original configuration. In its final version the Hawk lasted in US Army service until 1994. (*DOD*)

(**Above**) The replacement for the Second World War-era 105mm Howitzer M2A1 that was relabelled the M101A1 in 1962 was the 105mm Howitzer M102 pictured here. The latter entered into service beginning in 1964 and went on to see widespread use during the Vietnam War. Much lighter than its predecessor, the M102 could be transported by helicopter or be air-dropped by parachute. (*DOD*)

(**Opposite, above**) Another Second World War artillery piece that survived into post-war service with the US Army was the towed 155mm Howitzer M1, which was relabelled the M114A1 in 1962. Its replacement in 1978 was the towed 155mm Howitzer M198 pictured here. The weapon was air-transportable by the C-130 Hercules, but due to its weight and size was found at the XVIII Corps level and not organic to airborne divisions. (*DOD*)

(**Opposite, below**) In 1953 the army took into service the initial model of the MGR-1 Honest John Rocket. The rocket could be fitted with a conventional high-explosive (HE) warhead but was primarily intended to be fitted with a nuclear warhead. It was fired from a 6 × 6 M139 5-ton Truck referred to as a Transporter, Erector, Launcher (TEL) seen here. It began to be replaced in 1973 by the MGM-52 Lance. (*National Archives*)

(**Above**) The smallest tactical nuclear-armed weapon in service during the Cold War with the US Army was the M29 David Crockett Weapon System. It entered service in 1961 and remained in the inventory until 1971. Due to its small size it was air-droppable by parachute, along with its associated 4 × 4 0.25-ton truck fitted with a launcher unit. It was also carried in armoured personnel carriers but launched from the tripod shown. (*National Archives*)

(**Above**) To supplement the much larger and heavier MGR-1 Honest John Rocket and TEL, the army came up with the MGR-3 Little John seen here. It was primarily intended to fire a nuclear warhead-armed rocket, but could also be fitted with a high-explosive warhead. Due to its compact dimensions and light weight, it was air-droppable by parachute and could be transported by helicopters. (*National Archives*)

(**Opposite, above**) The post-war replacement in the army for the Second World War 6 × 6 2.5-ton Cargo Truck, better known as the 'Deuce and a Half', was the Model 35 seen here. Like its predecessor, it was a 6 × 6 2.5-ton Cargo Truck that came in numerous versions, each assigned a different designation. Early versions were gasoline-engine-powered, with later versions being diesel-engine-powered. (*DOD*)

(**Opposite, below**) In the late 1960s, to reduce costs the army began looking into replacing the specially-designed post-war M37 0.75-ton Truck, which entered service in 1949, with an off-the-shelf commercial vehicle. The eventual result of this process led to the fielding in 1967 of the vehicle seen here, designated the M715. The vehicle was a slightly modified Kaiser Industries J-Series Gladiator pick-up truck. (*Ian Wilcox*)

(**Opposite, above**) In its continued efforts to cuts costs, the army embarked upon a programme referred to as the Commercial Utility Cargo Vehicle (CUCV) series. The initial vehicles acquired, beginning in 1970, were Dodge products. These were replaced beginning in 1983 by General Motors products. A preserved example, seen here, was designated the M1009. (*Ian Wilcox*)

(**Opposite, below**) In the immediate post-war era, the airborne leadership continued to consider how a tank could be delivered to an objective along with its paratroopers. Experiments were conducted with the C-82 Packet and the M24 Light Tank pictured here. However, the tank could only be transported by disassembling it and delivering it via two aircraft and the army quickly lost interest. (*Pierre-Olivier Buan*)

(**Above**) The M56 90mm Scorpion SPAT (Self-Propelled Anti-Tank) pictured here was designed in the 1950s. It had a suitable gun for its intended purpose. However, to keep the vehicle's weight down so that it could be carried by existing transport aircraft, it had no armour protection. A total of 160 were built between 1957 and 1958, enough to equip the three airborne divisions in service at that time: the 11th, the 82nd and the 101st. (*Chris Hughes*)

(**Opposite, above**) The lack of any armour protection on the M56 90mm Scorpion meant that it was useless for offensive operations. To rectify that issue and take advantage of new anti-tank guided missile technology, a new tank programme was set in motion in 1956, known as the 'Airborne Assault Weapon System'. That eventually evolved into a series of pilot vehicles that first appeared in 1962, an example of which is seen here, labelled the XM551. (*Patton Museum*)

(**Opposite, below**) The first two production examples of what was now referred to as the M551 Sheridan 'Armored Reconnaissance/Airborne Assault Vehicle' (AR/AAV) came off the assembly line in July 1966. They first entered service with the army in 1967. Despite a host of serious design problems, never completely solved, it remained in the inventory long enough to see service during Operation DESERT SHIELD/STORM in 1991, as shown here. (*DOD*)

(**Above**) With the never-ending technical and design issues that bedevilled the M551 Sheridan, the army began looking into a possible replacement vehicle in the early 1980s, labelled the Armored Gun System (AGS). Among the firms that responded to the army's interest was the FMC Corporation, which came up with the prototype vehicle seen here, armed with a 105mm main gun. FMC named their submission the Close Combat Vehicle Light (CCVL). (*Author's collection*)

(**Opposite, above**) Teledyne Continental Motors came up with a very radical approach to meet the weight and size restrictions desired by the airborne forces in the AGS. Unlike the fairly conventional designed CCVL, Teledyne Continental's contending vehicle had the entire three-man crew in the rear hull, and a small external unmanned turret armed with a 105mm main gun as pictured here. The engine and transmission were in the front hull. (*Patton Museum*)

(**Opposite, below**) In 1987, it was concluded that the armoured protection on the CCVL and other contending vehicles was too thin, against the protests of the airborne forces (as this meant the vehicle would not be air-droppable) and that a more thickly-armoured vehicle was required. This would lead to the redesigned version of the CVVL seen here. It was eventually cancelled due to a lack of funding. (*FMC Corporation*)

(**Above**) With the lack of an adequate number of paratroopers by early 1969, the army came to realize that the 101st was an airborne division in name only. This led to the decision that the 101st should be converted into the army's second airmobile division in July 1969, the first having been the 1st Cavalry Division (Airmobile) converted in July 1965. The standard light troop transport helicopter at the time was any of the various models of the UH-1 'Iroquois', unofficially nicknamed the 'Huey', seen here. (*US Army*)

(**Opposite, above**) In this painting titled 'Helicopter Pickup' by Paul Rickets, soldiers of the 101st are portrayed evacuating a wounded comrade to a UH-1 Huey helicopter during the Vietnam War. The first version of the Huey showed up in South Vietnam in 1962, configured either as an ambulance helicopter or troop transport. The most numerous model of the Huey to see service in the Vietnam War was the UH-1H. (*US Army Center for Military History*)

(**Opposite, below**) Supplementing the UH-1 series Huey helicopters during the Vietnam War was the CH-47 series helicopter seen here, officially nicknamed the 'Chinook'. It first entered into army service in 1962 and found itself deployed to South Vietnam in 1965. As it was a much larger and more powerful helicopter than the UH-1 Huey series, the CH-47 could recover downed aircraft and transport artillery pieces.(*Paul and Loren Hannah*)

(**Above**) This museum diorama depicts a North Vietnamese Army anti-aircraft gun and crew during the Vietnam War. The 12.7mm machine gun was designated the DShK-1938/46. It was an improved version of a Second World War Red Army machine gun and nicknamed the '*Dushka*' (meaning 'Sweetie'). It was a serious threat to US Army helicopters throughout the Vietnam War. (*USAF Museum*)

To protect its slow and low-flying helicopters from enemy anti-aircraft guns during the Vietnam War, the US Army modified some of its existing inventory of transport helicopters as gunships, armed with machine guns and rockets. It was not long before the US Army solicited a specialized helicopter gunship. What they got was the AH-1 series named the 'Huey Cobra' seen here. (DOD)

To identify targets for the UH-1 Huey gunships and AH-1 Huey Cobras in South Vietnam, the US Army placed into service the OH-6A Cayuse and the OH-58A Kiowa. The latter remained in front-line service after the Vietnam War. In 1984, a new version appeared designated the OH-58D, which can be identified by its beach-ball-shaped Mast Mounted Sight (MMS) affixed above the main rotor assembly. (DOD)

The eventual replacement for the army's inventory of AH-1 series Huey Cobras was the AH-64 series officially nicknamed the 'Apache'. The first examples of the new helicopter came off the production lines in 1983 and entered front-line service in 1986. It has three main weapons: a 20mm automatic cannon in a chin turret, rocket-launcher pods on either stub wing, and the AGM-114 Hellfire anti-tank missile. *(DOD)*

The UH-1 series Huey helicopters performed yeoman work during the Vietnam War. However, approximately 3,000 were lost during the conflict. In 1972, the army issued requirements for a replacement helicopter that was far more capable and tough. The end result in 1977 was the UH-60 series 'Black Hawk' seen here in a painting by Al Sprague titled 'Air Assault, Tinajitas'. *(US Army Center for Military History)*

In this photograph we see a UH-60 series Blackhawk of the 101st being loaded onto a C-5 Galaxy. The helicopter first saw combat with the US Army during Operation JUST CAUSE (the invasion of Panama) in December 1989. Due to extremely heavy enemy small-arms fire during that operation, removable Kevlar armour blankets to line the passenger compartment were needed. (*DOD*)

Chapter Four

Post-Cold War

With the internal collapse of the Soviet Union on 8 December 1991 and the resulting end to the long-running Cold War, the US Army once again began a dramatic drawdown in strength. The 1989 Army of Excellence (AOE) had an active duty strength of 770,000 personnel and eighteen divisions, including the 82nd and the 101st. By 1995, the AOE had an active duty strength of approximately 500,000 and consisted of only ten divisions, including the 82nd and 101st.

Despite a great deal of study following the end of the Cold War on how to better prepare the AOE for a wider range of conflict categories, by 1999 the US Army senior leadership had decided that its heavy divisions remained too cumbersome to transport quickly, and the light divisions such as the 82nd and 101st lacked the staying power for sustained combat operations. By this time, the AOE TO&E received the label 'Legacy Force' and what the army was planning for the future found itself labelled the 'Objective Force'.

Big Changes in the Works

An important aspect of the Objective Force, eventually labelled the 'Future Force', was to leverage new information-age digital communication technology, and the much-improved situational awareness that it provided, to eliminate layers of the command structure.

The importance of digital information to the US Army appears in this passage from a US Army Center for Military History publication titled *Kevlar Legions: The Transformation of the US Army 1989–2005* by John Sloan Brown:

> The Pentomic Division of the 1950s sought to reduce vulnerability to atomic weapons by compressing battalion and brigade into a more nimble battle group. Among other flaws, the Pentomic design depended on communications capabilities that did not reliably exist at the time. By the 1990s space-based communications and digital technologies overcame this particular impediment. Widely-dispersed forces could communicate without recourse to matrices of ground stations, and huge masses of information passed through cyberspace – and the ether – in high-volume burst transmissions.

Another goal of the Future Force was to convert the entire army, not just its light forces, into a more expeditionary posture. Pushing this transformation process along came about as the US Army became involved in two major conflicts: one in Central Asia and the other in the Middle East.

Operation ENDURING FREEDOM

In response to the 11 September 2001 terrorist attack upon the Twin Towers of the World Trade Center in the United States, organized and carried out by the terrorist organization known as Al Qaeda, the American government decided to invade the country of Afghanistan, located in Central Asia. Its government, referred to as the Taliban, was considered unfriendly to America's interests and had allowed Al Qaeda to establish training bases in their country.

The American invasion of Afghanistan received the code-name Operation ENDURING FREEDOM-Afghanistan (OEF-A), which was itself considered part of something broadly referred to as 'the Global War on Terror'.

Reflecting the land-locked isolation of Afghanistan, the initial portion of the publicly-acknowledged military operation began on 7 October 2001 and consisted of aerial attacks by both American and British forces employing aircraft and cruise missiles. The ground phase of the operation was publicly acknowledged by the American military as starting on 19 October 2001.

The US Army's initial ground commitment to OEF-A consisted not of divisions, or even brigades; rather it was composed of small teams of multi-service Special Forces units. It was these units that quickly overthrew the Taliban government, with support from a number of anti-Taliban Afghan warlords. Unfortunately, those Taliban forces not killed or captured retreated to the Afghan countryside and, with secure bases in the neighbouring country of Pakistan, reformed and continued to threaten the early gains made by the American multi-service Special Forces units.

The Endless Battle for Afghanistan

To contain the resurgent Taliban, the US Army committed a brigade of the 101st in November 2001, followed on a rotational basis by elements of all the army's other divisions including the 82nd, which have continued through to today.

The Medal of Honor citation of Sergeant Ryan M. Pitts of the 173rd Brigade of the 101st for an action on 13 July 2008 provides an example of the fighting encountered by the airborne troopers and other US Army soldiers in Afghanistan:

> Early that morning, while Sergeant Pitts was providing perimeter security at Observation Post Topside, a well-organized Anti-Afghan Force consisting of over 200 members initiated a close proximity sustained and complex assault using accurate and intense rocket-propelled grenade, machine-gun and small-

arms fire on Wanat Vehicle Patrol Base. An immediate wave of rocket-propelled grenade rounds engulfed the observation post, wounding Sergeant Pitts and inflicting heavy casualties. Sergeant Pitts had been knocked to the ground and was bleeding heavily from shrapnel wounds to his arm and legs, but with incredible toughness and resolve, he subsequently took control of the observation post and returned fire on the enemy. As the enemy drew nearer, Sergeant Pitts threw grenades, holding them after the pin was pulled and the safety lever was released to allow a nearly immediate detonation on the hostile forces. Unable to stand on his own and near death because of the severity of his wounds and blood loss, Sergeant Pitts continued to lay suppressive fire until a two-man reinforcement team arrived.

From the public affairs office of the 82nd, released online on 12 March 2010, appears an extract describing the actions of Warrant Officer James Woolley during an engagement in Afghanistan that earned him a Silver Star:

In November 2009, Woolley and his crew were called for a casualty evacuation mission in Badghis province, western Afghanistan. As Woolley and his crew approached the pick-up site, his left door gunner reported heavy tracer fire coming at them. Woolley and his co-pilot maneuvered to avoid the rounds. Once they were able to land, ground troops began loading five wounded soldiers on the aircraft.

Very quickly, the aircraft began taking more enemy fire. With less than a minute on ground, insurgents fired a rocket-propelled grenade at Woolley's Chinook. The round penetrated the nose, flew between the two pilots, and hit the flight engineer in the back of the head before coming to a rest inside the helicopter, unexploded.

Woolley and his crew continued to take a barrage of enemy fire, but Woolley directed the team to stay on ground until the last patient was loaded. Once the fifth patient was loaded, Woolley led the team out of the hot landing zone and back to a coalition base where the casualties could receive treatment. After they determined the aircraft was still flyable, Woolley made the decision to conduct a second casualty evacuation of several wounded and dead Afghan National Army soldiers.

Despite the best efforts of the US Army soldiers like Sergeant Ryan M. Pitts and Warrant Officer James Woolley as well as the army's NATO multi-national allies, the Taliban could not be eradicated and continues to threaten the American-friendly Afghan government, established in December 2004, up until today.

The last NATO-contributed coalition forces withdrew from Afghanistan in December 2014, leaving the US Army to continue the fight. It was at this point that

Operation ENDURING FREEDOM received the new code-name of Operation FREEDOM SENTINEL.

Back to Iraq

On 20 March 2003, an American-led coalition of military forces invaded Iraq once again, with the bulk of the ground forces consisting of US Army divisions. The publicly-acknowledged reasons by the then American government for the invasion revolved around Saddam Hussein having weapons of mass destruction (WMDs) and having established ties with a number of international terrorist organizations. Subsequent detailed investigations by the American military showed that both reasons had been unfounded.

Both the 82nd and 101st would play a part in what became code-named Operation IRAQI FREEDOM. More so the 101st, as only a single brigade from the 82nd was assigned to the invasion force in case any opportunities arose for an airborne operation. A proposed parachute assault to capture Saddam International Airport near Baghdad by the 82nd and the 75th Ranger Regiment did not take place.

The Initial Fighting

As in DESERT STORM, the 101st was to use its fleet of helicopters to plunge deep into Iraq in an effort to outflank the Iraqi ground forces standing in the way of the army's heavy division's drive to Baghdad, the nation's capital. It did so by establishing a daisy chain of Forward Operating Bases (FOBs), allowing the division's attack gunships and those of other divisions free rein throughout Iraq.

To aid in defending its fleet of transport helicopters, the 101st made an unusual decision as seen in this extract from the 2004 US Army Center for Military History publication titled *On Point: The US Army in Operation Iraqi Freedom*:

> To provide security to the helicopter fleet, the 101st attached 136 door gunners to the 159th Aviation Brigade alone. The gunners came from the three maneuver brigades in the 101st Airborne Division after they had received a 40-hour block of formal training on aviation operations and aeromedical factors. Attaching infantry as door gunners not only supported security but also facilitated maintenance. With infantrymen serving as door gunners, only one crew chief flew with the aircraft during missions. The second crew chief remained behind and conducted ground maintenance on aircraft not assigned a mission. Thus, the division maximized the availability of its most maneuverable and responsive asset.

Roadblocks

An unexpectedly strong Iraqi resistance in the cities on the path to Baghdad began to delay the US Army's heavy divisions. The single brigade from the 82nd and brigades from the 101st found themselves assigned to clear those urban areas and secure the highways needed by the generally-unarmoured logistical tail of the heavy divisions.

From the US Army's official history of Operation IRAQI FREEDOM comes this extract describing the impressions of Major Michael Marti of the 82nd in the fighting for the Iraqi town of As Samawah on the morning of 30 March 2003:

> At the outskirts of the town the Iraqis, and perhaps some Syrians, employed suicidal attacks. In the city they fought house-to-house, employing human shields, and near the bridge over the Euphrates [river], the paramilitary troops employed RPGs [rocket-propelled grenade-launchers] fired in volleys and mortars registered on roads and bridges. Marti observed: 'They never changed the way they fought, so we were able to use appropriate tactics to counter. Fighting started at 0800 local every day and then stopped at 1800. It was like they were punching a clock like Wile E. Coyote in the cartoon.'

Another example of what confronted the airborne soldiers in the urban combat conducted in Iraq appears in the personal experience monograph of Captain Jason Davis of the 101st. The date is 4 April 2003 and the place is the Iraqi city of Karbala, located 60 miles south of Baghdad:

> The platoon ran into the building, the CO [commanding officer] and I last, covering each other. Once inside, the platoon got on the second story and then the rooftop. We could see for miles and soon discovered all of the enemy positions to our north and east. It was a shooting gallery. We decimated them. The locals kept coming out to watch; we yelled at them at first but soon discovered only warning shots fired generally towards them dispersed the crowds. It was like entertainment for these people to watch a battle going on. We began to realize that most of the enemy, who, at one time wore OD [olive drab] green uniforms, now wore civilian clothes. Crowd control took on a whole new meaning, as we attempted to distinguish combatant from spectator and spectator from spotter for enemy mortar fire. There were numerous repeat customers hidden amongst the civilian spectators, who we finally identified as spotters. We shot them. Events like this went on for hours. We fired over 100 rounds of 105 artillery and uncountable rifle rounds.

From the personal experience monograph of First Lieutenant Jason Wharton of the 101st appears this passage detailing his defensive actions during the fight to hold on to recently secured Saddam International Airport on the evening of 6 April 2003:

> As these attacks occurred, my squad leaders had difficulty identifying the enemy with their night vision capabilities. The terrain was sparsely wooded, but illumination was poor. Instead, we had to rely on our thermal capabilities and lasers to

point out suspected enemy locations. The PEQ-2A [rifle laser sight] and the Infantry in Battle 172 PAC-4C [rifle laser sight] were crucial in identifying enemy positions to subordinates. I also relied on the use of our new 60mm infrared illumination round to identify these enemy locations. Rather than allow the threat to close the distance on our locations, we began to call for and adjust 60/81mm mortar fires. The most effective combination proved to be a mixture of high-explosive rounds and white phosphorous ... The end result of this technique was a success. I did not deplete the mortar ammo, and my M203 [single-shot 40mm under-rifle-barrel grenade-launcher] gunners could mark targets with HEDP [high-explosive, dual-purpose] rather than focusing on illuminating the battlefield. In the morning, we realized that we had not destroyed the remnants of a platoon but the remnants of an infantry battalion.

The 101st eventually consolidated around Baghdad, which fell on 9 April 2003. Shortly after that it was ordered to northern Iraq and assumed responsibility for policing four provinces in north-east Iraq. The division returned to the United States in early 2004, as did the 82nd.

The Fiasco Unfolds

Unfortunately, the American government had badly underestimated the number of military personnel required to secure Iraq from further bloodshed. This had been pointed out by the outgoing US Army's chief of staff in February 2003, before the American Congress. His opinion was reaffirmed by a pre-invasion RAND Corporation report that had suggested the same.

The opinions of those who felt that the American military lacked the resources to secure Iraq once Saddam Hussein left power found themselves rejected by the then president and his staff. The result was that Iraq would be plagued by endless bloodshed requiring constant rotations over the years that followed by all the US Army divisions, including the 82nd and 101st, to help maintain the peace as best they could.

The large-scale American presence in Iraq would continue until 18 December 2011, when it officially concluded. Since that time, however, elements of the 82nd and 101st have continued to return to Iraq in both the advisory role and in minor combat roles, assisting the Iraqi military in its fight with the Islamic State (ISIS).

The Modular Force Appears

In response to the drain on its resources imposed by combat operations in Iraq and Afghanistan as well as the open-ended war on terror, the AOE was badly stressed. The US Army's senior leadership decided that a new organization structure and TO&E was required that was better suited to the demands then placed upon it.

An explanation of the major difference between those TO&Es that came before and the new TO&E appears in a passage from a US Army Center for Military History publication titled *Transforming an Army at War: Designing the Modular Force, 1991–2205* by William M. Donnelly:

> In September 2003, the U.S. Army began converting itself from an organization centered on divisions numbering from 10,000 to 18,000 soldiers to one based upon brigades totaling at most 3,900. The means for doing this became known as modularity, which the Army defined as a design methodology aimed at creating standardized, expandable army elements capable of being tailored to accomplish virtually any assignment. The new units would be as capable as their predecessors, but they would also be adaptable enough to assume whatever form was necessary to meet a broad range of missions.

Three types of modular brigades appeared in 2003, referred to as 'units of action'. Subsequently, they became the Infantry Brigade Combat Team (IBCT), the Stryker Brigade Combat Team (SBCT) and the Heavy Brigade Combat Team (HBCT). The latter re-designated as the Armored Brigade Combat Team (ABCT) in 2012.

The IBCT obviously possesses the highest level of strategic mobility of the three types of BCTs, but once on the ground, its main disadvantage is its poor tactical mobility. From a September 2010 US Army manual titled *Brigade Combat Team*, a passage describes the preferred combat environments for an IBCT:

> While IBCTs are optimized for offensive operations against conventional and unconventional forces in rugged terrain, their design also makes them capable in complex terrain defense, urban combat, mobile security missions, and stability operations. IBCTs are better suited for operations in restrictive and severely restrictive terrain than the other types of BCTs. This is true whether the enemy is conventional or unconventional and whether the mission is in support of operational maneuver or operations against insurgents.

The various types of BCTs that formed the core of the US Army's new modular force TO&E introduced in 2003 were all assigned to divisions, although divisions ceased being tactical commands then. Each division oversaw up to six brigades, plus their supporting units. The US Army's 3rd Infantry Division was the first to be restructured into the modular force TO&E beginning in 2003. The 101st began the process in 2004 and the 82nd in 2006.

The XVIII Airborne Corps continues to oversee the army's two airborne divisions, as well as the 3rd Infantry Division and the 10th Mountain Division, which has and remains the army's only light infantry division. Besides the XVIII Airborne Corps, the army also has two other corps, all of which fall under the oversight of the United States Army Forces Command (FORSCOM).

In addition to the 82nd and the 101st airborne divisions, there is based in Vicenza, Italy, the independent 173rd Airborne Brigade Combat Team, formed in 2003. Rather than FORSCOM/XVIII Airborne Corps control, it is under the oversight of the United States European Command (EUCOM).

Brigade TO&E

With the advent of the BCT concept, the different TO&Es of the airborne, air assault and light divisions that had evolved under the AOE were standardized, with all generally equipped and trained the same. Personnel strength was around 3,300.

Of the five brigades typically found in the 82nd or 101st, three are always IBCTs. They form the fighting core of the divisions and are considered manoeuvre brigades. Both the light infantry and airborne IBCT personnel are qualified to perform the air assault role when required. Another important brigade of an IBCT is the combat aviation brigade, also common to the two other types of BCTs.

Combat Aviation Brigade New Equipment

A new addition to the combat aviation brigade inventory of all the BCTs, beginning in 2003, was Unmanned Aerial Vehicles (UAVs). The first proved to be the ground-guided 'RQ-7 Shadow'. In 2009, the much larger 'MQ-1C Gray Eagle' appeared.

The Shadow has no weapons, but the Gray Eagle flies into combat with the 'AGM-114 Hellfire' fire-and-forget missile. The Gray Eagle receives directions in-flight from the AH-64 Apache helicopter gunship. It now performs the forward reconnaissance mission for the BCT combat aviation brigades. This led to the last version of the OH-58 series scout helicopter, named the 'Kiowa Warrior', retiring from the army inventory in 2017.

Recent Changes to the TO&Es

In previous division TO&Es the support elements, combat and combat service support were typically found at the divisional or corps levels. With the introduction of BCTs, which were in effect miniature divisions, the support elements, referred to as 'sustainment brigades', were pushed down to the brigade level command. This provided the BCTs with an unprecedented degree of autonomy and self-sufficiency.

In a change of heart, in 2016 the US Army decided that sustainment brigades and the field artillery battalions of the various types of BCTs would revert to divisional level command rather than the brigade level command as initially implemented in 2003. This came about as the US Army became convinced that they operated with increased efficiency at that higher command level. Once this occurred, the divisional level became a tactical command element once again, with the ability to direct fire onto an enemy. During the Second World War, the corps was the highest level of tactical command that could direct fire onto an enemy.

Battalion TO&E

The three manoeuvre brigades of the 82nd and 101st originally consisted of two infantry battalions each. In 2013, the army reduced the overall number of BCTs so that it could add a third infantry battalion to each of the remaining BCTs. This brought the personnel number in each IBCT to approximately 4,400.

Also included with each manoeuvre brigade are a single cavalry squadron (battalion) and a single field artillery battalion. The latter is organized to provide fire support and counter-fire. It has sixteen towed 105mm howitzers (M119 series) in two eight-gun batteries, each with two four-gun firing platoons. As of 2005, there is also a single battery equipped with eight M777A2 155mm towed howitzers.

Also there is an engineer battalion (formerly known as the special troop battalion) and a brigade support battalion in each IBCT. Depending on the mission or missions assigned, other BCTs can augment an IBCT, be it an SBCT or an ABCT, or elements from the other services, whether ground or air.

Company TO&E

The three infantry battalions of the post-2012 IBCT manoeuvre brigades of the 82nd and 101st have three infantry companies each, supported by a heavy weapons company. Each rifle company is further broken down into three rifle platoons, a weapons squad and a 60mm mortar section.

The headquarters company for each IBCT infantry battalion has a scout platoon, a sniper squad and a platoon of 81mm and 120mm mortars. The weapons company has four wheeled assault platoons, each with several wheeled vehicles armed with anti-tank guided missiles. These platoons provide stand-off protection against enemy armour for the IBCTs. In addition, the weapons company is armed with the M2HB .50 calibre machine gun and the Mk 19 40mm Grenade-Launcher.

The wheeled vehicles consisted of different versions of the High-Mobility Multipurpose Wheeled Vehicles (HMMWVs), better known to most by its unofficial nick-name of the 'Humvee'. As of 2016, the first production units of the Humvee's eventual replacement in front-line service, referred to as the Joint Light Tactical Vehicle (JLTV), rolled off the assembly line.

Reconnaissance TO&E

The reconnaissance squadron of the three IBCT manoeuvre battalions is composed of four troops: a headquarters troop, two mounted reconnaissance troops and one dismounted reconnaissance troop. The two mounted reconnaissance troops ride on Humvees. The dismounted reconnaissance troop is easily deployable by air.

Each of the mounted reconnaissance troops includes three reconnaissance platoons and a mortar section. The reconnaissance platoons have six Humvees. The mortar section consists of two towed 120mm mortars and a fire direction centre

(FDC). The dismounted reconnaissance troop includes a sniper squad and two dismounted reconnaissance platoons.

From a 2010 US Army manual titled *Reconnaissance Platoon* is this extract describing its battlefield functions:

> The primary mission for the reconnaissance platoon is to gain information and survey enemy territory. This is conducted as part of security, stability, and other missions; and can be performed mounted or dismounted. Mounted reconnaissance is conducted when time is critical, and there is a need to cover a large area quickly. This allows a fast tempo in combat that makes maximum use of the optics, firepower, communications, and protection provided by reconnaissance vehicles. Dismounted reconnaissance allows platoons to gather detailed information, enhance security, and move with stealth in rugged terrain.

The reconnaissance platoons have three sections with one fire-and-forget 'FGM-148 Javelin' anti-tank missile-launcher in each platoon. It was introduced into US Army service in 1996 and has proven itself as a multi-purpose weapon able to engage a wide range of targets.

Global Response Force

In 2007 the American Department of Defense (DOD) established the requirement for a military organization, with its leading elements, to be able to be transported anywhere in the world within twenty-four hours in response to military or humanitarian contingencies. That formation received the title 'Global Response Force' (GRF). Although intended as a multi-service arrangement, the nucleus of the GRF has been and continues to be the 82nd.

From an article in the July-August 2013 issue of *Military Review* magazine by Brigadier General Charles Flynn and Major Joshua Richardson titled 'Joint Operational Access and the Global Response Force: Redefining Readiness' appears this description of the 82nd's role in the GRF:

> The 82nd Airborne Division maintains the GRF. Organized to conduct combat operations as the lead ground element for a joint force land component commander, the GRF's mission is synonymous with the division's overarching mission to strategically deploy and conduct forcible-entry parachute assault to secure key objectives for follow-on military operations in support of U.S. national interests.

In addition to the organic assets of the 82nd, as part of the GRF it can be augmented on short notice with elements of other units. These can range from tanks to more specialized units such as explosive ordnance disposal (EOD) teams, a military police (MP) platoon, and additional engineer and military intelligence units. From the USAF a contingent consisting of a special tactics team, tactical air control parties and an air liaison officer is available, and from the US Navy a joint task force port opening team.

Despite the main roles for which it was intended, the United States Government Accountability Offices (GAO) identified some organization flaws with the GRF. One of these appears in an October 2017 report titled *Actions are Needed to Enhance Readiness of Global Response Force to Support Contingency Operations*:

> DOD has developed the GRF as a rapid response force available to react to unforeseen contingencies or crises. While the GRF has responded to worldwide contingencies, GRF units have been primarily used to augment existing geographic combatant command capabilities. DOD has not assessed the risks it assumes by its reliance upon the GRF for augmenting combatant commanders' forces as opposed to having the GRF-assigned units available for allocation to a joint task force in response to a contingency. Without performing a risk assessment and, as appropriate, designing responses to mitigate any identified unacceptable risks to accomplishing either of the two GRF uses, DOD cannot ensure that the GRF is able to meet its mission.

Continuing into service with the USAF until the present day is the C-130 Hercules series. Progressively improved throughout its service life, from 1992 to 1996 the C-130H model pictured here was produced, which featured new avionics as well as an integrated radar and missile warning system. An identifying feature of the H-model Hercules is the four-bladed propellers. (*DOD*)

(**Opposite, above**) Beginning in 1999, the USAF took into service the C-130J Super Hercules, which featured British-designed and built Rolls-Royce turbo-prop-driven engines instead of the traditional American-designed and built Allison turbo-prop-driven engines. The J-model of the C-130 series can be identified by its six-bladed propellers as is seen in this photograph. (*DOD*)

(**Opposite, below**) Paratroopers are packed into the cargo compartment of a C-130J Super Hercules which, like the earlier models in the series, was 40ft long and approximately 10ft wide. Ceiling height in the aircraft is 9ft. The C-130J Super Hercules can transport sixty-four paratroopers, while a stretched version labelled the C-130J-30 Super Hercules can transport ninety-two paratroopers. (*DOD*)

(**Above**) Originally considered as the replacement for the C-130 series, when finally introduced into full service in 1995, the C-5 Globemaster III proved to be the replacement for the then aging C-141 Starlifter and a partial replacement for the C-5 Galaxy series. Pictured here is the prototype C-17, which first flew in 1991 and revealed a host of serious design flaws that had to be resolved before production began. (*DOD*)

(**Above**) The C-17 Cargomaster is a much larger aircraft than the C-130 series as is evident in this picture, with a cargo compartment that is 88ft long, 18ft wide and 12ft high. The cargo compartment floor and that of the ramp are two-sided. For personnel and vehicles, it is flat on one side. There are rollers on the other side that are employed when the aircraft is carrying palletized cargo. (*DOD*)

(**Opposite, above**) Compared to the 64 paratroopers that the C-130H or standard C-130J Hercules could carry, the large and spacious cargo compartment of the C-17 Globemaster III seen here has room for 102 paratroopers. Unlike the C-141 Starlifter that required long paved runways, the C-17 can land and take off from short and small unpaved runways, although this does increase the odds of damage to the aircraft. (*DOD*)

(**Opposite, below**) Inside a C-17 Globemaster III a jumpmaster prepares to give the okay to a paratrooper to depart the aircraft. The large bag located under the T-11R reserve chute on the front of the paratrooper's lower abdomen is referred to as the Enhanced Parachutist Drop Bag (EPDB). It can hold anywhere from 35lb to 125lb of equipment. Like its Second World War counterpart, it is released by a paratrooper just before landing. (*DOD*)

(**Opposite, above**) To make sure that the palletized cargo intended for air-drops arrives at the correct spot without requiring that transport aircraft (such as the C-17 Globemaster III shown here) to fly low and slow over the landing zone and expose itself to enemy anti-aircraft defences, there is the army's Precision and Extended Glide Airdrop System (PEGASYS) and the USAF Precision Airdrop System (PADS). (*DOD*)

(**Opposite, below**) Inside the cargo compartment of a C-17 Globemaster III is palletized cargo, included two HMMWVs. The latest delivery method for ensuring that air-droppable cargo arrives where intended was debuted in 2006 and is referred to as the Joint Precision Airdrop System (JPADS). The system involves each air-droppable palletized cargo pod having an onboard computer connected to the Global Positioning System (GPS) and steerable parachutes. (*DOD*)

(**Above**) Paratroopers are shown here unpacking a palletized HMMWV after a training exercise. The C-130 Hercules series was capable of delivering palletized cargo, or even the M551 series Sheridan tank, via the Low Altitude Parachute Extraction System (LAPES). That requirement was dropped from the C-17 Globemaster III in 1994 by the US Army as the aircraft could not perform the role without serious re-design efforts. (*DOD*)

The army has both free-fall parachutes, as well as the MC-6 Maneuverable Canopy Parachute System. The standard paratrooper current parachute as of 2014 is labelled the Non-Maneuverable Canopy (T-11) Personnel Parachute System and is pictured here. It replaced the T-10 Parachute System, introduced shortly after the Korean War. *(DOD)*

The Non-Maneuverable Canopy (T-11) Personnel Parachute System seen in the arms of this paratrooper has an average rate of descent of 19ft per second compared to the older-generation T-10D, which was 24ft per second. This significantly lowers landing injury rates for jumpers. In addition, the T-11 has a unique deployment sequence to reduce the opening shock of the parachute deploying and the follow-on canopy oscillation. (*DOD*)

Since the Second World War, of crucial importance to paratroopers on reaching the ground has been reliable radio communications. The digital revolution as applied to today's radio technology has provided today's paratroopers as pictured here with a wide variety of options. These include Single Channel Ground and Airborne Radio System (SINCGARS) and Ultra High Frequency (UHF) Satellite Communications (SATCOM). (*DOD*)

A hold-over from the late Cold War era, and continuing to see productive service with the army, is the UH-60 Blackhawk helicopter pictured with a sling-loaded HMMWV. The most current models in service are the UH-60M and the UH-60V. More powerful engines in the UH-60M provide it with increased troop and cargo-carrying capacity. The UH-60V will update the older-model UH-60L analogue architecture to a digital configuration. (*DOD*)

The replacement for the Vietnam War-era SPH-4 helicopter helmet is the Star-Wars-looking helmet pictured here. It is referred to as the Aircrew Integrated Helmet System (AIHS). Introduced in 2014, it increases both head and hearing protection for the wearer. The visor protects the wearer from laser light and the face-shield a degree of protection from small fragments. (*DOD*)

This soldier wears the Advanced Combat Helmet (ACH) introduced into service in 2003. It was the replacement for the Kevlar helmet that formed part of the Personnel Armor System for Ground Troops (PASGT) introduced in 1983. The ACH weighs less than the Kevlar helmet, yet offers superior protection. In 2014, the army began to issue an even lighter version referred to as the Lightweight Advanced Combat Helmet (LW-ACH). *(DOD)*

In response to the ever-increasing toll of soldiers killed in HMMWVs by insurgents in Iraq and Afghanistan, the army sought ever heavier armoured HMMWVs, which continue to serve with the army until today as is seen in this image of an M1151 up-armored HMMWV (UAH), with the up-armour B-3 Kit. The paratrooper in the foreground is wearing a headset and microphone, as well as protective spectacles. *(DOD)*

(**Above**) The high losses among soldiers manning the machine guns on the roof station of the HMMWV armament carriers (in Iraq and Afghanistan) forced the army to develop ever more elaborate armoured turrets for the vehicles. The eventual answer was to take the soldier out of that position and replace them with the Common Remotely Operated Weapon System (CROWS) seen here. (*DOD*)

(**Opposite, above**) The latest version of the Tube-Launched-Optically-Tracked, Wire-Guided (TOW) missile system remains the mainstay of the army's airborne and light infantry divisions. In this image we see a soldier holding up a sealed disposable missile launch tube (containing a ready-to-fire TOW missile) that fits into the launcher unit mounted on the HMMWV armament carrier roof-mounted weapon station. (*DOD*)

(**Opposite, below**) Seen in this photograph is the one-man, electrically-driven, 360-degree rotating turret pod of the AN/TWQ-1 Avenger anti-aircraft missile system. It is mounted on the rear platform of an unarmoured HMMWV chassis. On either side of the turret pod are two launching units, each containing four Stinger surface-to-air missiles. The Avenger can fire its missiles from a halt or on the move. (*DOD*)

(**Above**) As the enemy in Iraq and Afghanistan turned to the widespread use of Improvised Explosive Devices (IEDs), the HMMWV, never designed to stand up to such a threat, was faring badly. The US Army's answer was the acquisition of a large number of specially-designed armoured trucks referred to as Mine Resistant Ambush Protected Vehicles (MRAPVs), some of which, like the example pictured in the foreground, continue to serve to this day. (*DOD*)

(**Opposite, above**) To aid in detecting conventional military mines as well as IEDs, the US Army fielded the Mine Protection Vehicle Family (MPVF), which consists of a variety of specialized wheeled vehicles of different sizes and types. Pictured in the foreground is the Husky Vehicle Mounted Mine Detection (VMMD) system, which is also considered a route clearance vehicle. (*DOD*)

(**Opposite, below**) In 1986, the US Army tested the US Marine Corps Light Armored Vehicles (LAV-25) for possible employment by the 82nd. For whatever reasons, the idea was not pursued. In 2016, the US Army decided to re-evaluate the LAV-25 for possible use by the 82nd and this time around concluded that it would be a valuable addition to the division. The vehicles went into service in 2017 as pictured here. (*DOD*)

(**Above**) Entering into production in 2015 for the US Army was the Joint Light Tactical Vehicle (JLTV), seen here in Afghanistan with the 82nd. It is the intended replacement for the army's current inventory of armoured HMMWVs as well as the Mine Protection Vehicle Family (MPVF). The JLTV has a much higher level of off-road mobility, fuel efficiency and reliability than the earlier generation of vehicles. (*DOD*)

(**Opposite, above**) Seen in this photograph, mounted on the rear cargo platform of a Joint Light Tactical Vehicle (JLTV), is the dedicated all-weather, twenty-four-hour, near-real-time, ground-based tactical signals intelligence and electronic warfare system referred to as 'Prophet Enhanced'. It is not platform-dependent, meaning that it can be configured to fit on a variety of vehicle types. (*DOD*)

(**Opposite, below**) In service with the US Army since 1996 is the Family of Medium Tactical Vehicles (FMTV), an example of which is pictured here. It comes in a wide variety of models, serving in many different roles, including as a weapons platform. There are two weight categories: the 2.5-ton Light Medium Tactical Vehicle (LMTV) and the 5-ton Medium Tactical Vehicle (MTV). (*DOD*)

(**Opposite, above**) First seeing employment with the US Army during the Vietnam War and still in service today as seen here during a training exercise is the Anti-personnel Mine M18A1 Claymore. It contains 700 small steel pellets encased in a plaster casting and weighs 3.5lb. It has a maximum range of 270 yards, although its effective range is listed as only 55 yards. (*DOD*)

(**Above**) Brought into service by the US Army during the Vietnam War as the replacement for the M14 Rifle was the M16 Rifle. It has remained in service with the army in progressively-improved versions. The paratrooper pictured here is adjusting the sling on his M4A1 Carbine, which was authorized as the standard carbine for the army in 2010. The bayonet is designated the M9. (*DOD*)

(**Opposite, below**) The US Army has progressively introduced a number of adaptors to the M4A1 Carbine, which allow it to be fitted with a variety of devices to improve its battlefield effectiveness. On the M4A1 Carbine pictured here the weapon has an optical scope mounted on the receiver, a laser aiming sight on the top of the forward hand-guard and a white light sight on the side of the forward hand-grip. (*DOD*)

Pictured here is the single-shot 40mm M320A1 Grenade-Launcher. It can be mounted underneath the front hand-guard of an M4 or M4A1 Carbine or employed as a stand-alone system as pictured here. It has a maximum effective range of 437 yards. In its stand-alone configuration the M320 weighs 6.48lb and when attached to an M4 or M4A1 Carbine only 3.42lb. (DOD)

Combat experience gained in Iraq and Afghanistan showed that the US Army's M4A1 Carbine, firing a 5.56mm round, lacked the range and stopping power to kill enemy combatants at longer ranges. This led the army to reissue in limited numbers the M14 Rifle, taken out of service during the Vietnam War, to some of its soldiers as shown here. Its 7.62mm rounds possessed the knock-down power to kill the enemy at longer ranges. (DOD)

Looking to replace the M24 7.62mm Sniper Weapon (SWS) the US Army adopted in 2008 the M110 7.62mm Semi-Automatic Sniper System (SASS) shown here. Besides its employment as an anti-personnel weapon, it is also classified as a light anti-matériel weapon. It is normally fitted with a 3.5-10 × scope seen in the picture, which provides the weapon with a maximum effective range of 875 yards. (DOD)

In 2010, the US Army began an upgrade project using its existing inventory of the M24 7.62mm Sniper Weapon System (SWS), which had first entered service in 1988. The newest version of the M24 is designated the M2010 Enhanced Sniper Rifle (ESR) and is pictured here. It comes with a suppressor and has been re-chambered to fire the more powerful .300 WinMag ammunition. (DOD)

The most powerful sniper rifle in the US Army inventory is the M107 Semi-Automatic Long-Range Sniper Rifle (LRSR) pictured here. It is a commercial product that was rushed into service for Operation DESERT STORM in 1991 and has remained a potent specialized weapon in the army's arsenal. It fires a .50 calibre round out to a maximum effective range of over 1,000 yards. *(DOD)*

The M249 5.56mm Squad Automatic Weapon (SAW), introduced into US Army service in 1984, has been modified and upgraded based on user community input and continues to serve. New features include a plastic collapsible butt-stock as pictured here, in place of the original fixed plastic butt-stock. There is now a 200-round cloth pouch instead of the original 200-round hard plastic case shown. *(DOD)*

The latest version of the M249 5.56mm Squad Automatic Weapon (SAW) in service with the US Army and optimized for airborne/air assault soldiers is the short-barrel model pictured here, sometimes nicknamed the 'Para' version. Mounted on the adaptor rail, fitted to the weapon's receiver, is the M145 Machine Gun Optic (MGO) allowing machine-gunners to engage targets at extended ranges. (*DOD*)

This soldier from the 101st in Afghanistan is armed with the 7.62mm M240B Machine Gun that first appeared in US Army service in the late 1990s. In its original configuration it was accepted in army service in 1977 as a coaxial machine gun for various tanks and armoured fighting vehicles. It was the proven durability of the weapon mounted on vehicles that resulted in it being adapted for infantry use. (*DOD*)

Desiring a lightweight version of the 27.3lb 7.62mm M240B Machine Gun, the US Army began fielding the M240L pictured in 2010, which weighs only 21.8lb. The weight saving was achieved by using a titanium receiver and alternative materials for fabricating the major components of the weapon. The M240L also features a shorter barrel than the M240B. *(DOD)*

Continuing in service with the US Army into the twenty-first century is the tried and true M2 .50 Caliber Machine Gun pictured here. In post-combat surveys soldiers rate the weapon among the most effective in their small-arms arsenal. The latest model in use today is designated the M2A1 and has a quick-change barrel and fixed headspace and timing. It also comes with a new flash-hider that makes the weapon less detectable in darkness. *(DOD)*

First entering into US Army service in the early 1980s is the Mk 19 Grenade Machine Gun pictured here. It weighs 77.6lb without a mount or tripod. When engaging point targets, its 40mm grenades have a maximum effective range of 1,640 yards and when engaging area targets, it can effectively take them under fire at up to 2,419 yards. (*DOD*)

US Army soldiers on a range have just fired an M3 Multi-Purpose, Anti-Armor, Anti-Personnel Weapon System (MAAWS). It was first introduced into army service in 2011 for use in Afghanistan. It is a Swedish-designed 84mm recoilless rifle best known to most as the 'Carl Gustaf'. Empty, the weapon weighs 36lb and has a maximum effective range with a rocket-boosted round of 1,094 yards. (*DOD*)

(**Above**) Impressed by the battlefield performance of the M3 Multi-Purpose, Anti-Armor, Anti-Personnel Weapon System (MAAWS) in Afghanistan, in 2018 the army took into service a lighter and shorter version designated the M3A1 seen here. It comes with an adaptor rail on the top of the weapon for fitting a variety of optical sights, including a red dot sight. (*DOD*)

(**Opposite, above**) To maintain the battlefield effectiveness of the Tube-Launched, Optically Tracked, Wire-Guided (TOW) anti-tank missile system into the twenty-first century, it has constantly been improved over the decades that it has been in US Army service. The latest version pictured here is now referred to as the Close Combat Missile System-Heavy (CCMS-H) TOW. (*DOD*)

(**Opposite, below**) Another anti-tank weapon in US Army service since 1996 is the FGM-148 Javelin pictured here. It was the replacement for the M47 Dragon anti-tank missile system. Rather than being wire-guided like the Dragon, the Javelin is a fire-and-forget missile. To avoid the back-blast associated with recoilless weapons, the Javelin has a soft-launch system, with the missile flight motor not ignited until a safe distance down-range. (*DOD*)

(**Above**) The 60mm M224 Mortar introduced into US Army service in 1978 has been replaced by an improved model seen here in action, designated the 60mm M224A1 Lightweight Mortar. It weighs 13 per cent less than the previous version yet retains all the capabilities of the earlier model. It can also be operated by one man in direct fire when fitted with a smaller base plate. (*DOD*)

(**Opposite, above**) The US Army began replacing its Korean War-era 4.2in (107mm) Mortar M30 with a new Israeli-designed 120mm mortar in 1991. That foreign-designed mortar was labelled the M120, with an improved version seen here designated the M120A1. It is towed into action and operated by a five-man crew. With a sustained rate of fire of four rounds per minute, it has a maximum effective range of almost 8,000 yards. (*DOD*)

(**Opposite, below**) The 1989 replacement for the 105mm Howitzer M102 in US Army service was the British-designed 105mm Howitzer M119 seen here. The latest model is the M119A3, which first entered service in 2013. It features software and hardware component upgrades, a Global Positioning System (GPS), a digital gunner's display and digital communication between each gun of a battery and its fire-direction centre. (*DOD*)

(**Opposite, above**) Introduced into US Army service in 2005 was the towed Lightweight 155mm Howitzer System (LW155) pictured here. Extensive use of titanium in the construction of the LW155 meant that it was 7,000lb lighter than its predecessor, the towed 155m Howitzer M198. The LW155 has a Digital Fire Control System (DFCS) and an inertial navigation system, with a Global Positioning System (GPS) back-up. *(DOD)*

(**Above**) Pictured here are two examples of the towed Lightweight 155mm Howitzer System (LW155) being transported by the latest version of the CH-47 Chinook series in US Army service labelled the F-model. This version has an upgraded digital cockpit, a monolithic airframe and vibration damping. To operate in adverse flight conditions the CH-47F comes with a digital automatic flight control system. *(DOD)*

(**Opposite, below**) In this image we see the US Army's man-portable Lightweight Laser Designator Range-finder (LLDR). It was designed for day-and-night, all-weather use. Soldiers employ the LLDR to acquire, precisely locate and engage targets with precision Global Positioning System (GPS)-guided and laser-guided munitions, and also improve the effectiveness of engagements with unguided munitions. *(DOD)*

(**Above**) The latest version of the AH-64 Apache helicopter gunship in service with the US Army is the E-model pictured here, with the Mast-Mounted Sight (MMS). Armament consists of up to sixteen fire-and-forget Hellfire anti-tank missiles, seventy-six 2.75in rockets and 1,200 rounds of 30mm ammunition for its chain gun. One of the key design features of the E-model is its ability to control drones, known as Unmanned Aerial Vehicles (UAVs). (*DOD*)

(**Opposite, above**) On a US Army flight line is the last of the OH-58 Kiowa series helicopters that originally debuted during the Vietnam War. In the configuration pictured here it was labelled the OH-58D Kiowa Warrior and armed with machine guns and rockets. In a cost-saving measure, the army decided to retire its fleet of OH-58D Kiowa Warriors in 2016. Its role will be taken over by the AH-64E Apache, working together with UAVs. (*DOD*)

(**Opposite, below**) In this picture a paratrooper holds a very small reconnaissance drone referred to as the RQ-11B Raven Small Unmanned Aircraft System (SUAS). It has a wingspan of 4.5ft and weighs 4.2lb. The range of the drone is approximately 6 miles, with an aerial endurance of 120 minutes at 500ft or higher. It is intended for use by battalion commanders and below. (*DOD*)

Soldiers prepare for a mission a mid-sized drone labelled the RQ-7Bv2 Shadow Tactical Unmanned Aircraft System (TUAS). Launched with the aid of a towed ramp, the drone is intended for employment by Brigade Combat Teams (BCTs), has a range of 31 miles and can remain in the air for up to eight hours. It is capable of working in conjunction with the AH-64E Apache helicopter gunship. (DOD)

The largest drone in US Army service is the turbo-engine prop-driven MQ-1C Gray Eagle Unmanned Aircraft System (UAS) shown here. It is a division-level asset that offers commanders a long-endurance platform with wide-area surveillance capability. In addition, the drone can conduct target acquisition and act as a communication relay, as well as conduct attack missions. (DOD)